Amazon used £3.95

C000058901

# BRITISH FOREIGN POLICY
## CENTU

5274

# British History in Perspective
General Editor: Jeremy Black

# BRITISH FOREIGN POLICY IN THE TWENTIETH CENTURY

## C. J. BARTLETT

**MACMILLAN**

© C. J. Bartlett 1989

All rights reserved. No reproduction, copy or transmission of
this publication may be made without written permission.

No paragraph of this publication may be reproduced, copied or
transmitted save with written permission or in accordance with
the provisions of the Copyright, Designs and Patents Act 1988,
or under the terms of any licence permitting limited copying
issued by the Copyright Licensing Agency, 90 Tottenham Court
Road, London W1P 9HE.

Any person who does any unauthorised act in relation to this
publication may be liable to criminal prosecution and civil
claims for damages.

First published 1989 by
MACMILLAN EDUCATION LTD
Houndmills, Basingstoke, Hampshire RG21 2XS
and London
Companies and representatives
throughout the world

ISBN 0–333–43769–1 (hardcover)
ISBN 0–333–43851–5 (paperback)

A catalogue record for this book is available
from the British Library

Printed in Hong Kong

Reprinted 1992

# CONTENTS

In loving memory of my wife, Shirley

# INTRODUCTION

JAMES JOLL has suggested that we may have to resign ourselves to a 'kind of two tier history' – at one level 'the broad lines of social and economic development', at the other 'the decisions of individual leaders' which might profoundly affect the course of events in the shorter term, or perhaps even for a decade or two. In recent years the first level has begun to attract increasing attention from students of British foreign policy, a development exemplified in two thought-provoking books, *The Realities behind Diplomacy* by Paul Kennedy, and yet more radically by Bernard Porter in *Britain, Europe and the World*. At the same time controversy has continued to flourish among scholars over the minutiae of decision-making, so that the detailed conduct of British foreign policy during the years leading up to both world wars, in the Cold War, and in Britain's post-war relations with the United States, Western Europe and Afro-Asia has all been subject to examination, re-examination and criticism from widely differing angles and points of view.

Various approaches to the study of British foreign policy in the twentieth century are thus feasible, and each is replete with controversy. The present work is deliberately selective, with a definite bias towards high politics, or the more traditional approach. For Joll's first 'tier' the reader should turn initially for more detailed analysis to Kennedy and Porter, though any study directed at the second 'tier' must of necessity draw upon their work and that of the many scholars who have begun to deepen our knowledge of the influence of domestic politics and of diverse social and economic forces upon the policy-makers. No analysis of the controversies surrounding British foreign policy-making is possible without reference to the varied constraints and pressures to which those who took the crucial decisions were subjected, and only by so doing can one begin to suggest answers to questions on their range of choice and, within that range of choice, the appropriateness of their responses and subsequent conduct. By so doing it may be possible to chart a course between the conflicting currents represented by such scholars as Keith Wilson and Bernard Porter. Where the latter sees little freedom of action, arguing for instance that there was little that Sir Edward Grey could have done to alter the course of events leading to 1914, Wilson retorts: 'There was no inevitability about the content of British foreign policy. Nothing need have been as it was. There were always alternatives. There always are.'[1]

Those with experience of authority at the highest level have sometimes commented on the extent to which the power at their disposal fell short of their eager expectations as they climbed the 'greasy pole'. As early as 1895 Lord Salisbury commented: 'Governments can do so little and prevent so little nowadays. Power has passed from the hands of the statesman, but I should be very much puzzled to say into whose hands it has passed.' Some sixty years later Anthony Sampson embarked upon a search for 'the sources of power', analysing in the process individuals as well as institutions. He concluded that 'the rulers' were not to be found at the centre of a solar system. Indeed there was no real centre, only 'a loose confederation of institutions . . . compounded not so much of hard round balls of material advantage, as of vague clouds of moods and feelings'. He discovered muddle rather than order, with means often receiving more attention than ends. Yet he still reached the interesting conclusion that 'in the age of the common man . . . much of the history of our time has been forged by a handful of men'.[2]

Christopher Thorne takes one of the most controversial examples of British policy-making in this century – the era of appeasement in the 1930s – and suggests that scholars may have gone too far in substituting 'helpless men' for 'guilty men'. In a more positive context Kenneth Bourne reminds us that policies 'have by their nature their own momentum and the paths of power and glory often tend to diverge. In such circumstances the direct and usually sudden inspirational intervention of a statesman ... alone seems able to restore the harmony of purpose.'[3] Naturally one cannot separate the statesman from his times, and it has been argued, for instance, that even Lord Salisbury, so often acclaimed for his intellectual and detached approach to foreign policy, was greatly influenced by his personal identification with the interest of the landed aristocracy in low taxation. This concern reinforced his preference for a peaceful and relatively inexpensive foreign policy.[4] On influences of this kind, and on *innenpolitik* in general Zara Steiner remarks that almost everything begins to seem relevant. Yet in the end, whatever the vulnerability of those in authority to outside pressures, their subjective responses to and their selective interpretations of the information before them are crucial. The personal element in decision-making cannot be ignored even when the constraining forces may seem overwhelming.

While it may seem improbable that alternative decisions and strategies could have significantly lessened Britain's relative decline in the world of the twentieth century, the courses of action – and inaction – chosen by Britain profoundly influenced developments in Europe and many other parts of the world. This was especially true of the first half of this century, but remained so to no small extent thereafter. With so much at stake British foreign policy therefore should be approached in neither too deterministic a frame of mind nor with exaggerated notions of what the British might have been able to achieve if only they had acted with sufficient vigour and imagination.

# 1
# PARTIAL COMMITMENT AND TOTAL WAR

AT FASHODA on the Upper Nile in 1898 the British achieved their last relatively inexpensive major success in foreign policy. An isolated France was unable to withstand her old opponent's determination to secure undisputed control of the Sudan and so confirm Britain's position in Egypt. In reality, however, even this was only a local triumph – it could not reverse the growing feeling of unease among those who reflected on Britain's changing position in the world. They recognised that it was becoming increasingly difficult to preserve the extensive empire and influence which the British had been carving out for themselves, notably in the last 150 years, helped by the distractions and weaknesses of others. Even Lord Salisbury, prime minister, foreign secretary and exponent of the 'free hand' in the late-nineteenth century, was not immune to such worries. At the end of his life he too was expressing doubts about the adequacy of past policies in the face of new challenges – though whether these were imminent or more distant he did not pretend to know.[1] Lord George Hamilton, at the start of the new century, had no doubts: 'it will require men of exceptional capacity, resolution and tenacity to bridge over the time in which we shall pass from the old position we occupied in the nineteenth century to that which . . . the British Empire ought to occupy in the twentieth.'

Britain in 1900 was a small, densely populated island, heavily dependent upon cheap food and raw material imports. It paid for these with manufactured exports and invisible earnings. The wealth of the nation as a whole, the income of rich and poor alike, and hence the very stability of British society, were dependent upon their continuance. In an increasingly competitive world, while protectionism might have had its theoretical attractions, the majority of the population believed that free trade was the better safeguard of the existing standard of living – notably through the provision of cheap food. Cheap imports in general also helped to restrain wage costs for the benefit of British exports. Additions to the empire were compatible with free trade, and the empire as a whole was seen both as an immediate and a long-term economic asset. Furthermore it provided outlets for emigrants and varied forms of employment from the humblest to the highest in the land. In so far as opinions varied about the costs as opposed to the benefits of empire, habit, pride, belief in the military value of India, coupled with the conviction that Britain would cease to be a first class power without the empire, all worked in favour of the continuation of existing policies and attitudes. As a leading journalist, J. L. Garvin, remarked, 'the process has gone too far to be reversed'. When Salisbury's successor, Balfour, quietly observed that the loss of India might help to reduce taxation in Britain, he was indulging in no more than an academic aside. More pertinent at the time were such assumptions as Salisbury's description of India as an oriental barrack from which 'we may draw any number of troops without paying for them', or Curzon's insistence, with all the authority of a viceroy of India, that without the subcontinent Britain would become a third-class power. In any case it was widely expected that the challenges to Britain would multiply in the new century, especially once the United States and Russia with their vast territories, human and material resources began to realise their full potential. Perhaps a continental European or a Far Eastern power might also find a place in this emergent premier league of great powers. Britain in contrast would have to struggle to avoid relegation.

Yet if new measures were required for the defence of Britain's position in the world it was not easy to see how a people who had become accustomed to moderate levels of taxation, to

2

reliance on voluntary recruitment for the armed forces (and especially for the army), to a parliamentary system of government, and to modestly rising living standards among much of the working class as well as the middle and upper classes, could be persuaded to accept higher taxes, conscription and perhaps protectionism as part of a wider movement towards a more centralised and unified empire. Nor was there any disposition within the dominions to support the grand ideas for imperial federation propounded by enthusiasts such as Joseph Chamberlain. Only the Royal Navy enjoyed an exceptional position in the hearts of the British people. Naval supremacy was an agreed national interest (a consensus which was only partially modified by the anxiety of some Liberals and social reformers to promote the cause of arms limitation among the leading powers).

Admittedly the Declaration of London of 1909 (on neutral rights and contraband of war) has been singled out by Bernard Semmel as a potential threat to Britain's ability to control enemy and neutral merchant shipping in time of war, and as an example of the danger of the influence of misguided radicals and Liberals in Britain. Yet the same author concedes that 'many naval officers as well as ministers presiding over the Admiralty saw the agreements . . . as mere words to be abandoned if Britain became a belligerent'.[2] In fact the Declaration was not ratified, and its clauses were speedily ignored by Great Britain in the First World War. In so far as British economic warfare against Germany between 1914 and 1917 was restricted, this arose primarily out of respect for the world's greatest neutral, the United States – a power which once at war itself soon forgot its own principled defence of 'the freedom of the seas'.

But if British sea power was safe from enthusiastic do-gooders, there remained vested interests, national prejudices, traditional instincts, and a preference for *ad hoc* solutions, all of which combined to impede other efforts to enhance British security. It is obvious, however, that even given the will and a different outlook, and on the doubtful assumption that considerable success had attended such bids for greater national and imperial 'efficiency', Britain's resources would still have fallen short of her needs. Either way the British were heavily reliant upon skilled and inventive diplomacy and statecraft. In particular they faced a developing situation where it was tempting to conclude that many of the assumptions and methods of the last century were no longer appropriate and that some departure from the policy of the 'free hand' was imperative.[3]

Yet one traditional resource was husbanded with special care. The cost of the Boer War heightened the Treasury's determination to obstruct further impairment of Britain's precious ability to finance a major war more easily than her rivals. By 1900 finance was moving from a 'background influence to that of inescapable determinant' in British foreign policy.[4] In this pursuit of retrenchment from 1901 even the claims of the Admiralty were not immune to critical scrutiny, and the cabinet decided that, given the presence of six other major naval powers in the world, Britain had perforce to plan selectively. Priority was therefore given to building against the navies of Russia and France, and it was on the strength of their fleets that the two-power standard continued to be based. The navy was expected to improvise if the calculated gamble on satisfactory relations with any of the other four states failed to pay off.

This anxiety to nurture Britain's economic strength as an arm of defence in the event of war coincided with widespread fears of the damaging effects of any great war whether Britain was directly involved or not. The dislocation of markets would affect British industry and trade, and – perhaps with the hardships experienced by Lancashire during the American Civil War in the 1860s in mind – it was natural for many to assume that more than business profits would be at risk. Unemployment might generate serious working-class unrest. From this there followed the hope in some quarters that, if by some mischance, Britain became caught up in a major war, her role would be a strictly limited one. The more business could flourish 'as usual', the less the effect on the economy, and the smaller the threat of internal disturbances.[5] Once war with Germany seemed imminent in 1914 the foreign secretary, Sir Edward Grey, shared the dismay of the City of London at the likely economic consequences. He sought consolation in the belief that Britain would suffer little

4

more injury by participation than by standing aside in a position of degrading neutrality.

This does not mean that economic interests, both national and individual, always acted as a restraining influence on British policy. Thus British diplomats and consuls were prominent, for instance, in the scramble for economic concessions in China in the late 1890s, just as they had joined in the scramble for territory and other advantages in Africa earlier in the century. Even so they failed to satisfy many of those with extensive business interests in China. These aggrieved merchants wanted more. Yet the inability of the 'Old China Hands' to persuade the government to establish a virtual British protectorate in the Yangtse region is a classic illustration of the limited influence which a narrow group of businessmen could normally expect to exercise unless they had the support of other powerful economic or political interests working to the same end. The government in this instance was able to defend its policy of selective support with the argument that the prospective trading and investment opportunities in China did not justify more comprehensive action. Similarly Lord Cowdray later found that his oil interests in Mexico had to take second place to the Foreign Office's desire to avoid a collision with the United States for broad reasons of state. Admittedly it is not always easy to disentangle economic from other motives in a specific policy, any government having its own interest in the promotion and protection of British overseas economic influence. But clearly what also told against the 'Old China Hands' in the late 1890s was the higher priority which Salisbury accorded to the conquest of the Sudan (1898) and the government's decision to risk war with the Boers in 1899. Paramountcy was deemed imperative at key points guarding the route to India. Salisbury deliberately tried to limit rivalry in China in those years to facilitate success in Africa.

Salisbury's basic assumption, however, that a dangerous combination of European powers against Britain was improbable, unless the British themselves were guilty of some major provocation, was increasingly questioned by many of his colleagues. The sense of isolation during the Boer War strained many nerves. Growing economic and other challenges from Russia, Germany and even the United States, not to mention the traditional rivalry with France, encouraged reappraisals of traditional policies. The Boer War both tempered the jingoism of the later 1890s and, as noted already, strengthened the advocates of financial retrenchment in the cabinet. Renewed emphases upon the consolidation of the empire – formal and informal – and upon the removal of sources of friction with other powers wherever possible were the natural consequences. The sense of insecurity and loss of confidence were such that, whereas Salisbury had been content to pursue limited accommodations with Britain's leading rivals, his successors were prepared to go much further down that road, even if – as they initially believed – they were entering into partial rather than comprehensive commitments. It was under the influence of such considerations that an alliance and two ententes were negotiated between 1902 and 1907.

The full significance of these new developments was not always immediately appreciated by their creators, and, similarly, strong as were the inducements for the policy-makers to try to reduce the number of Britain's enemies, these did not necessarily determine with whom or to what effect Britain would negotiate. Initially the cabinet was eager to explore a variety of ways forward. Policy was experimental as well as shaped by individual preferences. Furthermore, fears that the policy of the 'free hand' had become a luxury were more potent influences than, for instance, simple Francophilia or Germanophobia. It is thus dangerous to take too deterministic a view of the outcome, and to be guided unduly by the knowledge that Britain and Germany would be at war from August 1914. The contemporary evidence does not sustain the argument that Britain was simply reacting to the activities of Germany. The latter's adoption of a policy of *weltpolitik*, or overseas expansion, from the mid-1890s did not make the triple entente, and therefore perhaps the First World War, inevitable.[6]

Indeed British interest in an understanding with Germany – pioneered so forcibly by Joseph Chamberlain in 1898 – was still alive in 1901, and persisted a little longer in the minds of some ministers. The deliberate exclusion of Germany from any great-power deal affecting the future of Morocco, a country increasingly

6

vulnerable to foreign intervention, was not initially British policy. What did become increasingly apparent in the course of 1901 was that in the area where the British were most in need of German support – namely in China – Berlin was not prepared to burn its fingers on their behalf. Germany's price – if indeed she ever seriously contemplated a deal – was a British commitment in Europe (against Russia and France) at a time when any sort of peacetime European commitment was an anathema to the British. Although Britain and Germany frequently found themselves in competition with each other, it was the difficulty of finding sufficient common interests which was much the most significant barrier to an agreement at the beginning of the century. This problem would have existed even in the absence of German interest in the creation of an overseas empire.

The British fared a little better in their approaches to the United States in that, while no positive support from that country was assured or even likely in return, it seemed sensible to placate this burgeoning power. Concessions could be made in the New World at no great expense to vital British interests (although the same was not true of Canada). It was equally reasonable to anticipate that the Americans would not exploit Britain's difficulties were she to come into conflict with another power. Russia, in contrast, posed problems of a very different order and magnitude, but here too Lord Lansdowne as foreign secretary from 1900 was eager to offer an olive branch. With their Central Asian railways advancing relentlessly towards the states bordering India, the Russians were causing Britain more immediate worries than any other rival power. They, however, had as yet no reason to allay British fears in Persia or Afghanistan. Among all the powers only Japan, overshadowed by Russia in the Far East, had an incentive to draw closer to the British at this time. But to Lansdowne Japan at first seemed a far from adequate partner, especially if an alignment here increased the risk of collision with Russia and perhaps, in consequence, with her ally, France. Not until he was convinced that no progress could be made either in Berlin or St Petersburg was Lansdowne able to discover some merit in talks with Tokyo. By the summer of 1901 the Admiralty was even more eager to negotiate. It saw in an alliance with Japan the quickest solution to Britain's current naval inferiority to Russia and France in the Far East. Armed with these and other arguments Lansdowne was finally able to persuade a somewhat reluctant cabinet to conclude a treaty with Japan in January 1902.

Ian Nish questions the conventional view that the alliance was a major departure from past policy.[7] Certainly it was not regarded as such in informed circles at the time. In any case it entailed no commitments outside China and Korea, and could be invoked only if one signatory was at war with more than one power. But ministerial hopes that it would make for peace and stability in East Asia were not realised – or not in the way that the cabinet had intended. The alliance increased Japanese self-confidence, thus making some – possibly a decisive – contribution to the outbreak of the Russo-Japanese War in 1904, a war whose repercussions were to be felt as far away as Europe. It is with these effects in mind that J. A. S. Grenville, for instance, has criticised the alliance as the first of several steps which increasingly circumscribed Britain's freedom of action. The Russo-Japanese War contributed significantly to the more definitive division of Europe into two camps.[8] The first signs of rigidity in British policy were apparent even before the end of 1903 when, out of loyalty to their ally and fearful of weakening this new link, the British failed to preach restraint in Tokyo despite the growing danger of war. This is not to say that the British were sufficiently Machiavellian to encourage a Russo-Japanese war, as suggested by the Soviet historian A. L. Galperin.[9] But Balfour did see war as an acceptable risk given his belief that a Japanese defeat (which many expected) would still compel Russia to station large forces in East Asia to prevent a Japanese resurgence. Nor was the cabinet tempted by the arguments of some in the War Office that a Russo-Japanese War might be the ideal moment to try to eliminate the Russian threat from Central Asia. It was equally deaf to the pleas of the viceroy of India, Lord Curzon, for a forward policy. The government wanted peace, and, in so far as it took a strongly anti-Russian line, it did so for defensive reasons.

Nor was it simply restrained by considerations of expense. In

1905 Lord Esher, a man whose modest official posts in no way reflected his influence in government from the king downwards, brooded uneasily over the degree of popular commitment to any war in defence of India. In a chilling phrase he suggested that among the public the subcontinent would not be considered 'worth a shilling [5p] on the Income Tax, or the lives of 50,000 street-bred people'. Doubts such as these, together with other weaknesses, go far to explain the nervous, often impulsive character of British diplomacy in these years. Nevertheless such considerations still have to be seen in the detailed context of the times. They influenced the general direction of rather than the specific decisions made by British governments. Thus the internal problems of Morocco, which did so much to precipitate the entente with France, at first found Lansdowne decidedly averse to 'the intended plundering of Morocco by the French'. The foreign secretary, like leading service personages, could also see advantages in a German-built Berlin–Baghdad Railway. This might add to the restraints on Russian influence in the Middle East. But the possibility of an Anglo-German understanding on this project was frustrated by Joseph Chamberlain and other anti-German elements in Britain. Furthermore, when the deteriorating situation in Morocco brooked no further delay at the end of 1902, it occurred at a time when Anglo-French relations were in a much happier state than those subsisting between Britain and Germany. There was a further inducement for Lansdowne to talk to the French when he learned that they were at last prepared to make concessions to the British in Egypt.

The pace at which Britain and France converged was also hastened by the deepening crisis between their respective partners in the Far East, Japan and Russia, in the second half of 1903. As early as 3 July there were hints from Paris that, in the right conditions, France might be able to restrain Russia or stand neutral in any Russian quarrel with Britain. Just how much fear of war in the Far East contributed to the conclusion of the entente in 1904 is not, however, easily resolved. Ian Nish accepts that it was 'unquestionably one factor', but is less satisfied than G. W. Monger, for instance, that it was a major cause.[10] Certainly account must be taken of those at the time who wished to capitalise on the opportunity to secure British interests in Egypt and simultaneously to find a solution to the Moroccan question which would not impair British security in the western Mediterranean. Keith Wilson, moreover, is most impressed by longer term considerations. He argues that the most powerful incentive impelling the British to conclude the entente was the hope that France, as the ally of Russia, might 'be disposed to bring about the primary goal of British foreign policy since the late 1890s: an agreement with Russia'.[11]

The different interpretations offered by modern historians are in themselves a reflection of the differing priorities as well as the divergent preferences of those who contributed to the making of policy at the time. Some scholars also detect here a qualitative change from the era of Lord Salisbury. His successors, it is claimed, failed to develop an equally comprehensive and sophisticated conception of Britain's power, interests and place in the world. Thus J. A. S. Grenville argues that where Salisbury had tried to establish a balance between ends and means, this was 'a quality not easy to detect in the policy of ill-defined commitment in Europe followed for two generations by succeeding Foreign Secretaries'.[12] Lansdowne, in his opinion, was guided more by expediency than by principle, or, as Zara Steiner contends, he was influenced by events and he 'never fully understood the consequences of his actions'. S. R. Williamson agrees that Lansdowne underestimated the impact on Germany even if he expected some retort over Egypt and Morocco.[13] In addition he failed to anticipate the serious consequences which followed from his acceptance of a clause in the 1904 agreement binding London and Paris to provide reciprocal diplomatic support for the terms relating to Egypt and Morocco, a strange oversight in view of past German interest in both territories. Too much attention, it seems, was given to the advice of Lord Cromer, the British consul-general in Egypt. And in the final analysis Lansdowne himself was lacking in statesmanship when he thought Berlin guilty of 'effrontery' when it drew attention to German interests at both ends of the Mediterranean.[14]

Lansdowne's record after the conclusion of the entente in April 1904 is a mixed one. Given that the Russo-Japanese War took so many unexpected turns, he could hardly have foreseen that by 1905 Germany would not only be in a position to exploit Russian weaknesses, but would do so in pursuit of more than a minor diplomatic victory in Morocco at the expense of France. Indeed, Germany chose to test the strength of the Anglo-French entente as well as the Franco-Russian alliance. The growth of the German navy added to British nervousness. Yet, interestingly and despite the periods of tension in 1905, Lansdowne did not resign himself to a permanent rift with Germany. Similarly, although the British armed forces around this time began to make serious contingency plans for a war with Germany, and although Lansdowne himself acknowledged that in certain circumstances Britain might have to stand beside France, he did not anticipate his successor's determination to support France – almost without regard for the immediate circumstances. There is nothing to suggest in the last months of Balfour's Unionist ministry in 1905 that the British were entering into staff talks with the French. Where Lansdowne did show weakness was in his failure to find at least a partial corrective to the rise within his own office of a new generation of influential bureaucrats who craved more certainty in Britain's foreign relationships than either he or Salisbury had thought necessary. These men were to find a staunch ally in Sir Edward Grey, Lansdowne's successor as foreign secretary.

Given the composition of the Liberal Party, with its strong radical wing, it was a matter of some consequence that a Liberal Imperialist such as Grey was appointed to the Foreign Office and should stay there during the remaining years of peace. Indeed another Liberal Imperialist, Lord Rosebery, who had opted for early retirement, strongly opposed the policy of entente. He protested in 1912 that 'no Glasgow merchant would do what we do in foreign affairs and that is, to engage in vast and unknown liabilities'.[15] These 'liabilities' were also worrying to the radical wing of the Liberal Party, although they were as much or more concerned with Grey's failure to challenge the conventional wisdom of the day – the secret diplomacy, the balance of power, the arms build-up and everything that perpetuated the system of power politics. This second group of criticisms

11

no longer excites much attention, but in other respects Grey's tenure of the Foreign Office remains as controversial as ever. Bernard Porter, with his emphasis upon forces beyond the control of diplomats, is prepared to make some excuses for the foreign secretary. Grey was the 'slave of pressures and of circumstances [beyond his control] and cannot be held fully responsible for a policy whose failure he felt deeply'. Britain, by the 1900s, faced an inescapable dilemma which conditioned her (and Grey's) response. But there are others who will not allow him to escape so lightly. Grey, it is argued, was not sufficiently alive to the destructive forces and emotions which were at work in Europe in the years leading to 1914. Keith Wilson criticises the rigidity of his mind. This meant that alternative policies from 1905 were not explored. Others have made the same point without going on – as Wilson does – to insist that Grey 'can be given no credit for the duration of peace between the Great Powers' down to 1914. Basically he followed a policy of containing Germany to preserve the friendship of France and Russia, thus adding significantly to the sense of frustration which prevailed in Berlin.[16]

At the heart of the argument lies the issue of 'partial commitment', brought into being by the ententes with France and Russia. Radicals at the time objected to the bias against Germany. They asked why, if Britain could negotiate with the detested tsarist autocracy, could she not settle her differences with the much less autocratic and more civilised state of Germany. On the other hand, and especially after the outbreak of war, there were those, usually on the right, who complained that 'partial commitment' was or had turned out to be a disastrous half-way house. Peace would have been assured had Germany been made to understand that Britain would range herself unequivocally beside France and Russia in the event of a crisis. In any examination of the possible alternatives to Grey's policy a necessary first step must be an attempt to clarify the reasoning behind the British reliance upon the two ententes. Some of the problems associated with that with France have already been discussed. Much more controversial is the origin of the agreement concluded with Russia in 1907, and Britain's use of both ententes thereafter.

It might seem at first sight that the elaborate calculations of British diplomats and strategists were of little moment beside the growing power and ambition of Germany, especially given the naval challenge from that quarter, and when Britain's foreign interests as a whole continued to exceed the resources which could be deployed in their defence. Vested interests at home would allow Britain neither to diminish her foreign commitments nor to protect them properly. The British, it might appear, were driven to seek partners out of necessity and, given the challenge from Germany, they had no option but to court Russia and France. Diplomats might devise refined arguments and sophisticated hypotheses, but in the final analysis it was these simple, brutal facts which prevailed. Yet in practice, as seen by contemporaries, Germany was not the only problem. Indeed between 1905 and 1914 she was not invariably the main problem. Agreements were needed to restrain partners as well as draw strength from them. Little, if anything, could be taken for granted at home or abroad. Grey and his advisers could not forget that they might be let down by cabinet, Parliament and the public at home, as well as by the nations abroad with whom they had concluded treaties, limited or otherwise. They worked on a beach where their sandcastles were always being threatened by encroaching tides. Evasion could become a normal means of communication. And in all this they still aspired to maximise the nation's freedom of action even if the so-called era of 'splendid isolation' had gone for good.

An understanding with Russia had been a major British objective even before the sharp deterioration in relations with Germany in 1905–6. Until then, as David Gillard observes, Britain's basic international worry (from 1885) had been the Russian threat to the north-west approaches to India, a threat compounded by Russian railway-building in Central Asia. The fear was not so much of a Russian invasion as of a concentration of Russian strength in or bordering on Persia and Afghanistan which the British could not match, and which might so denude British India of troops that the door was opened to a nationalist uprising. Whatever the justification for these fears they persisted as the War Office failed again and again to find a military solution. Hence the recurrent efforts to test the Russian readiness to negotiate in this sensitive area, and hence too the modifications to the Anglo-Japanese alliance in 1905. Britain and Japan were now treaty-bound to assist each other against only one belligerent. A war between Britain and Russia had not seemed impossible in 1904 (when Russian warships fired on British trawlers in the North Sea), while repeated British soundings in St Petersburg only began to elicit a positive response after Russia's defeat by Japan in 1905. The concurrent Russian revolution also had its effect. Even so opinion changed slowly and reluctantly in St Petersburg until talks were finally allowed to proceed on the issues in dispute between Britain and Russia in Afghanistan and Persia. The entente, as concluded in 1907, provided for the division of Persia into three spheres: the Russians in the north, the British in the south, with a neutral zone in between. It is worthy of special note that any Russo-German differences were of marginal importance in persuading the Russians to agree to such terms. On the British side, however, the motivation was more complex and is open to more than one interpretation.

The orthodox view is that the British government was now mainly preoccupied with the German threat. G. W. Monger expresses it thus:

> Grey's own statements leave no doubt that his chief motive in seeking a Russian entente was to change the balance of forces in Europe and in particular to create a counterpoise to Germany.[17]

But other scholars, to varying degrees, take note of the persisting fears of the Russian threat to India. Grey himself warned that Russia would recover in time from the disasters of 1904–6 whereas he did not believe the means and will existed in Britain to mobilise sufficient reinforcements to meet a great emergency in India. Thus Zara Steiner stresses the importance of the Russian as well as the German challenge. She argues that the primary wish of the British cabinet was to stabilise the situation in Persia and Central Asia, but there also existed 'the question of containing Germany in Europe . . . . [This] new link also completed Britain's changed orientation from an imperial to a European framework.' Consequently the threat to Britain's imperial position encouraged European involvements until the quest for a balance against Germany became 'the main focus' of Grey's policy.[18]

A much more radical thesis is developed by Keith Wilson. For him the Russian threat continued to be the main justification for the entente.

> It may seem that the involvement of Britain in a Franco-German war [during the Moroccan crisis in 1906] was a high price to pay for a chance to make an agreement with Russia, . . . It may seem, therefore, that the decision to seek such an agreement can only be accounted for in terms of the balance of power in Europe. This impression would, in my opinion, be false; like the Agreement with France, that with Russia was made not for the sake of the balance of power in Europe but for the sake of Britain's own Imperial interests.[19]

Only the fear of isolation as a result of a forfeiture of the French entente and the hope of building a bridge to Russia, in Wilson's view, can explain Grey's conduct. Anglo-German differences in 1906, 1908 and 1911, arising out of disputes in Morocco, were of insufficient moment in themselves to warrant war. Once he had concluded the entente with Russia Grey clung to it primarily to control the Russian threat to India.[20]

There is no lack of evidence to support Wilson's claims concerning the importance of Russia. During the Algeciras conference early in 1906 Grey specifically included Britain's relations with Russia among the reasons why Britain should not stand aside in the event of a Franco-German war. If that happened 'Russia would not think it worthwhile to make a friendly agreement with us about Asia'. At the same time, however, it should be noted that Grey also argued that if Britain failed to support France her reputation would suffer grievously in the eyes of *all* the other powers.[21] Furthermore he articulated his fears of Germany as a threat in her own right. He noted her current military advantages in Europe, thus making the present the worst possible moment for a collision. In time, however, there was 'at least the prospect' of an improvement in Britain's relations with Russia. If at some later stage it seemed desirable to check Germany's ambitions effective action might then prove possible. He admitted, however, that Germany might strike before such a combination could be created.[22] Only France and Russia were equipped to fight Germany on land, although Britain would play her part at sea. It is true that Grey could see additional advantages in the re-establishment of Russia as a counter-weight to Germany in Europe in that this would require a diversion of Russian strength from Central Asia. But the extent to which Germany preyed on his mind – as it did upon those of many others, especially in the Foreign Office and the armed forces – is evident in the contemporary documentation.

Documents of course, cannot always be interpreted literally. Many from these years offer ample scope for subtle textual criticism and lively debate. Dispatches and minutes may also bear the imprint of the emotions and special needs of the moment even when addressed to longer term problems. But Grey, despite his reputation for evasiveness, surely provides important clues in his minuted opinions on Germany. At times he suggested that Germany, overtly or covertly, was working towards 'a coming struggle with England'.[23] He oscillated between immediate and longer term fears. At times he seemed to regard the German naval programme as the only real issue dividing the two powers; at another he could complain of the unpredictability of the Kaiser – 'a battleship with steam up and screws going, but with no rudder'. And, it must be said, he could display as much concern at the overall consequences of losing the ententes as at any specific threat from Germany. As he once remarked, 'the one and only barrier which prevents Germany from being on satisfactory and good terms' with Britain and France was her determination to break the entente.[24]

Grey's varied interpretations of the German threat suggest genuine concern, but also some uncertainty about the immediacy of any direct German challenge to Britain. Not surprisingly some historians have come to question whether Anglo-German differences were as substantial as they appeared or were said to be. Zara Steiner heads a chapter 'The Myth of Rivalry?', and asks why was there 'perpetual talk of an impending war between Britain and Germany when there was nothing concrete to fight over?' This was particularly true of commercial and colonial

16

issues. Admittedly Germany's naval build-up was bound to cause concern, so fundamental was the principle of naval supremacy in British grand strategy. Yet Zara Steiner very fairly concludes that 'the Foreign Office tended to respond, not in terms of the actual challenge, but in accordance with its reading of Germany's ultimate intentions'.[25] Eyre Crowe, the noted Foreign Office expert on Germany, acknowledged in his famous memorandum of 1 January 1907 that there were no questions of any importance then in dispute. He wondered how far Germany was pursuing a planned policy of aggrandisement, or whether, as seemed more likely, it was mainly 'the expression of a vague, confused and unpractical statesmanship, not fully realising its own drift'. Often his most specific charge against Germany was his conviction that she could not be trusted. He further admitted in 1907 that the alternative of a Russo-French predominance would be as injurious to Britain, if not more so.[26] Hardinge, the permanent under-secretary, contributed a truly Bismarckian touch of his own when he commented that the more active Russia became in the Near East the more she would 'find herself in conflict with Germany and not in opposition to us'.[27] What better than for two of Britain's rivals to fall out among themselves?

The argument has also been propounded that much of the intense diplomatic activity of the British, with their insistence on an important role for Britain in the maintenance of the balance of power, arose from the belief that the nation required a defensive smoke-screen to obscure its relative weakness, especially in Europe.[28] Due attention was undoubtedly given to the cultivation of an appropriate British image abroad, and this took many forms. It was clearly among Grey's objectives when he took such pains to impress the Russians with Britain's concern for Serbia in 1909 in the closing stages of the Bosnian crisis – otherwise hardly a prime British interest. At the same time, whatever the Foreign Office's perception of Britain's place in the European balance of power, it was profoundly influenced by its own image of Germany. Thus Hardinge made the highly revealing comment in 1909 that Britain could not side with the Central Powers under any foreseeable circumstances: such a 'combination of England, Germany and Austria would not be

17

durable since it would imply the domination of Germany in Europe, and would inevitably end in war between Germany and England, the latter power being in a position of complete isolation and without even the sympathy of any of the Powers.' Grey agreed. Crowe reiterated this belief on the eve of war in 1914 when he recalled the fate of Prussia after she had stood aside from the war against Napoleon in 1805 only to fall victim to the Emperor a year later.[29] Here, surely, is evidence of a feeling that the inexorable logic of power politics was at work. Germany was feared because she was strong.

This sense of entrapment is highlighted by the occasional expressions of interest in alternative policies. Often as Grey insisted that the ententes were vital to prevent a return to what he described as Britain's exposed position before their creation, he too hankered occasionally after a less restricted range of options. His overtures to Germany after the Agadir crisis in 1911 were not simply the result of protests from within the Liberal Party. Grey remarked in April 1912, with a touch of exasperation, that 'Russia and France both deal separately with Germany, and that it is not reasonable that tension should be permanently greater between England and Germany than between Germany and France or Germany and Russia'. Nicolson as permanent under-secretary wrote rather airily at this time:

> We have a very simple policy, not to tie our hands in any way with anyone, to remain the sole judges of our action, to keep on the close terms we have hitherto maintained with France and Russia, and which have been the best guarantee of peace, while being perfectly friendly with Germany and ready to discuss amicably with her any pending questions.[30]

This was an idealised sketch of British policy and one which could have been elaborated only by the cultivation of a more consciously detached stance by Britain. As matters stood it was possible to believe in its accuracy only in periods of relative tranquillity between the powers.

This is borne out by the under-secretary's own reflection in April 1912 that an unfriendly Russia or France would be 'far more disadvantageous' to Britain than an unfriendly Germany. Although the latter could give Britain 'plenty of annoyance', it

18

could not really threaten 'any of our more important interests, while Russia especially could cause us extreme embarrassment, and, indeed, danger, in the Mid-East and on our Indian frontier'. Eyre Crowe himself gave an ostensibly even-handed warning, when war seemed imminent in 1914, that Britain – if she remained neutral – would place herself at the mercy of whichever side prevailed.[31] The growing rigidity in British policy after the departure from office of Lansdowne was thus confirmed (yet Lansdowne himself at the time of Agadir in 1911 and in August 1914 was as emphatic a supporter of the French entente as his successor). There occurred an instinctive reaffirmation of the importance of the ententes whether the threat came from Germany or from Britain's entente partners.

Only in 1913–14 did Grey and one or two of his advisers appear more open-minded. Thus, when trying to control the tensions which followed the First Balkan War (1912), or when discussing the future of Portugal's colonies and the Berlin–Baghdad railway with Germany, Grey seemed eager to believe in the existence of a moderate group in Berlin with whom it might be possible to do business. This helps to explain his too ready assumption for much of July 1914 that Germany could be relied upon to restrain Austria after the Sarajevo assassination.

Although historians in general are wary of talking of the development of some sort of detente in Anglo-German relations by the early months of 1914, account must be taken of Grey's readiness to explore, if not so much to act on, some new lines of thought. Admittedly, at the very same time, Russia's reviving power and ambitions excited so much concern, especially in 1914, that Grey and the foreign service argued even more strongly in favour of the ententes as still the most effective way to restrain Russia. Similarly there were lingering fears that Russia and Germany might once again draw together. Overall, as David Gillard has pointed out, a 'sequence of crises in Asia around 1912–14 were as much on the cards as a sequence of crises in Europe'.[32] Or so it seemed to the policy-makers. At the same time both Grey and General Sir Henry Wilson (a leading figure in the Anglo-French staff talks directed against Germany) were alive to the fact that Germany would fully share and probably

19

surpass their own concern at any significant revival of Russian power. Anti-German feeling in France similarly caused unease. Any new thinking in London, however, was abruptly halted by the decisions of Germany and Austria–Hungary in July 1914 to take matters into their own hands. There was thus neither the time nor the opportunity for the ideal situation to develop wherein the four continental powers tended to cancel each other out and, furthermore, so absorb each other's energies that little was left over with which to trouble the British outside Europe.

To claim that British policy from 1902 was relatively successful in that it reduced the task of the armed forces to 'a manageable size' is therefore only partially true – contemporaries lived in a state of recurrent alarm that their policies and calculations were about to be upset.[33] Britain could not give unqualified priority to Europe or to the empire until others decided on the venue of the next great war. This same conclusion also begins to provide an answer to the assertion that Britain would have served Europe better had she tried to act as a truly disinterested upholder of the European balance of power. She should, it is claimed, have paid more attention to the fate of the Habsburg Empire whose growing sense of insecurity was the most obvious threat to the peace of Europe.[34] Given such a premise the Foreign Office undoubtedly failed to treat the Austrian question with the seriousness it deserved. A rare spark of statesmanship had been supplied by Grey in 1908 when he refused to encourage Austrian separation from Germany in case this drove Germany to some act of desperation. Here at least he worked for a 'fair equilibrium'. Yet to have done more would have required a degree of confidence in British and imperial security which did not exist.

The criticisms offered by J. A. S. Grenville are more astute in that he acknowledges this lack of confidence even if he believes it to have been misplaced. In so far as he accepts British vulnerability both within and outside Europe, he believes the wrong remedies were applied. British policy, he suggests, was more closely related to German *Realpolitik* than has been generally recognised. Britain from 1902 was relying for safety upon the Bismarckian policy of balanced tensions between the powers (a fair description as long as it is accepted that the British fell short of Bismarck in ingenuity and imagination – creative or otherwise). Grenville goes on: 'Successful *Realpolitik* presupposes a degree of prescience that no statesman, not even the most experienced and talented can hope to possess over the longer term.' The future is too uncertain. 'What the years before 1914 show is how a loss of confidence and fear for the future can be as dangerous to peace as a naked spirit of aggression.' He doubts if the German threat to Britain was sufficient to justify the policy which was pursued by Grey and his colleagues.[35] Again this is true in part, although it could be said that in the end British fears and precautions were amply vindicated by German conduct in July– August 1914. Furthermore, whatever Britain's contribution from the 1890s to the frustration of German ambitions, and therefore to the do-or-die mood which was so poisonously influential and pervasive in Berlin by July 1914, the immediate fears and ambitions which tipped the balance in Germany in favour of risking war owed relatively little to Britain. Indeed, in so far as German leaders took account of Britain, they still hoped for her neutrality. Nor can one readily believe that any British concessions to Germany outside Europe would have put an end to German naval ambitions or – more importantly – to the resolve to preserve Germany's military lead over France and Russia – by war if necessary.

The apparent eagerness with which war was greeted in Britain in August 1914 has led some historians to ask whether Britain, too, provides evidence to support the argument that increasing internal tensions within the states of Europe were a major (even the major) cause of the First World War. Fritz Fischer in particular has developed this theory in the context of Wilhelmine Germany, and it has been stated more generally by the American historian, Arno Mayer. Rapid modernisation, according to Mayer, eroded the influence of those working for political and social compromise at home. The resultant polarisation between the forces of 'order' and the forces of 'change' tempted conservatives to try to strengthen their position in domestic politics by more aggressive foreign policies and if necessary by 'diversionary wars' to excite nationalist passions and a sense of national unity. In 1970 Arthur Marwick wrote of a growing crisis in liberal

England by 1914. 'Everywhere there was bellicosity, signs of a will to war.'[36]

It is true that Germanophobic and scaremongering groups had long been active, with sections of the press behaving in an unashamedly jingoistic and alarmist manner. Their influence and representativeness are more questionable. Doubt, for instance, has been cast on the strength of working-class support for the Boer War, while A. J. A. Morris – in a revealing study of the 'scaremongers' – notes both the presence of important divisions within the radical right and the dependence of the militants for success upon moderate and pragmatic groups which genuinely believed that British security or interests were at risk. Indeed those advocating arms limitation, the promotion of international law and international harmony were often more prominent. Thus James Joll concludes that, when all the domestic influences acting upon British foreign policy are aggregated, those working for peace conclusively outweighed those making for war.[37] These included powerful financial interests in the City of London, while Grey himself was at one with those who feared the effects of war upon the British economy – and consequently upon British internal stability. Before 1914, to 'whatever degree Grey felt threatened by the eclipse of his class and values, it made him more insistent on the need to avoid war through the application of reason and good sense'.[38] But these could not stand alone without some physical backing, so that in so far as Grey felt under pressure from outside opinion, he was evidently more embarrassed by his Liberal and radical critics than by pressure from the right.

While admittedly more study of the determinants of popular attitudes and of the growth of anti-German feeling in, for instance, the Conservative Party is required, the sheer strength of national feeling which could surface in response to a perceived threat to British security – and on an issue such as the German invasion of Belgium – must be accepted. R. C. K. Ensor, a pre-war critic of Grey, later conceded: 'The liberals had been making it an article of party faith [before 1914] that militarist Germany was not so black as it was painted. Now in a flash it seemed to be self-revealed as much blacker.' Radical faith in the superiority of many aspects of British civilisation helps to explain this *volte face* once Germany was identified as the immediate threat.[39] The minority of ultra-patriots in the Foreign Office, the armed forces, the press and the Conservative Party could not, of themselves, rouse a people satiated by conquest. But these people would respond to what they perceived to be a direct challenge. Many were also fired by continuing faith in the British mission in the world and by the righteousness of the British cause.

But until Germany's actions began to cause widespread alarm, Grey, for domestic political reasons, could not immediately announce Britain's wholehearted support for France – still less support for Russia. Yet for him it was unthinkable that Britain should stand aside given the assumptions which had guided his policy for so long. Hence his resignation warning – while the issue remained in doubt in the cabinet – if Britain failed to support France against a German attack. Britain's credibility and his own reputation were at stake. His position, however, was rapidly strengthened by the impact of German conduct on opinion in Britain. The Conservatives were increasingly aroused against Germany, and it was evident that if Grey chose to resign he could bring down the Liberal government. A coalition of pro-entente Liberals and Conservatives was the likely outcome. Thus Liberals who hesitated at the beginning of August faced a stark choice: they could either stand by France if the latter were attacked, or deliver power into the hands of a coalition ministry (dominated by the Conservatives) to fight the war in their stead.

In practice the German decision to take the offensive in the west, and especially Germany's flagrant defiance of Belgian neutrality in order to facilitate her attack on France, enabled most of the cabinet to choose war with a reasonably clear conscience. Yet the ambiguity and hesitation of several ministers offered a striking contrast to the single-minded views of those professional diplomats who were advocates of pure *realpolitik*. For them it was inconceivable that Britain should stand aside from a European war. If they thought a German victory most likely, they argued that almost any conceivable outcome was likely to result in British isolation and increased vulnerability. Britain had to fight in order to preserve her links with Russia and France. Without these she would lack the necessary influence over these partners and rivals to protect her interests both in Europe and in the wider world. It is significant that soon after the outbreak of the war even the far distant and fixedly neutral Americans began to expand their navy as a safeguard against whichever powers proved victorious in the European conflict. They too were succumbing to the apparent logic of power politics.

Britain, it would seem, had as little chance of avoiding participation in war in 1914, given her past decisions and the way the crisis developed, as she had of exerting influence over the course of the crisis itself. It is therefore only when they take the period 1905–14 as a whole that historians can develop effective arguments against Grey's conduct of foreign policy. Yet where Zara Steiner and others have described it as stubborn, imprecise, and lacking in understanding of the destructive forces which were at work in Europe, Grey's defenders insist that circumstances obliged the foreign secretary to pursue a policy of evasion and ambiguity, a policy which effectively promoted British interests until decisions were taken in European capitals over which he could exert little or no influence.[40] Those who regret the departure from the older policy of the 'free hand', or who suggest that Britain should have been more active as a mediator in Europe are balanced by those who warn that such policies would have demanded strong nerves, a readiness to run risks with British interests outside Europe, and a willingness to incur a heavier defence burden. Indeed, given that in 1914 the causes of the crisis lay in the heart of Europe, and that Germany's leaders were guided primarily by continental calculations, it would seem that only the prior existence of a British conscript army, readily deployable in France and Belgium, might have supplied the British government with the means to avert war.

In popular parlance the 1914–18 war was fought to end all wars. Rather more specifically at the level of government it became a war fought to establish permanent security against a resurgence of German militarism. Germany had to be denied a second chance to bid for hegemony in Europe. In fact, however, British policy-makers, especially the more astute among them, were not exactly sure what this would entail. In any case history would not come to 'a full stop' with the defeat of Germany. Consideration had therefore to be given to the wider implications to the balance among the powers in the event of a permanently weakened Germany.

Within the Foreign Office there was a tendency to blame and to try to identify the German 'war party'. Victory appeared to require the rooting out of Prussian militarism together with the imposition of such drastic social and political reforms as would guarantee the emergence of a peace-loving Germany. Among the British military the aims were often more modest. For them victory was needed to persuade Germans in general that war did not pay: they should be punished and intimidated rather than forced to transform their society. Lloyd George's thoughts occasionally went further. A lasting peace was essential, and among the prerequisites was the need to acknowledge that a 'great nation like Germany must live'.[41] At the same time in both civilian and military circles there were those who feared that Russia and perhaps France might emerge too much strengthened from the war. Thus Sir William Robertson, chief of the imperial general staff (1915–18), believed that a strong but chastened Germany might make a vital contribution to the future European balance of power. Contributions to the same end were sometimes expected from the Habsburg and Ottoman empires. Indeed the British initially hoped that the war would not spread to the Ottoman Empire, despite the latter's alliance with Germany, and when it did they tried to ensure that any Allied gains would not be at the expense of British interests in the Middle East.

The war years thus provide additional support for those who argue that Anglo-German relations must be seen in the context of Britain's global interests. Even the wartime Far Eastern gains of Britain's ally, Japan, caused some uneasiness. Similarly, the longer the war went on the more policy-makers began to fret at the growth in American influence. The greater, too, would be Britain's dependence upon that burgeoning country. Some Americans were fully aware of these possibilities, and it was due to the limited political skills of President Woodrow Wilson and to the reluctance of his mostly inward-looking countrymen to finance an expensive foreign policy from 1919 that the British escaped the worst of post-war competition from that quarter.[42] Finally, although the war ended with Russia torn by revolution and civil war, British ministers and service chiefs could not forget the pre-war importance of that power. What might not Russia become again – whether under Red or White rule?

Although war is the continuation of policy by other means, the work of diplomats does not cease. Grey and the Foreign Office ensured that the trade of the great neutral, the United States, was handled with more delicacy in the opening stages of the war than the Admiralty and Churchill would have liked. The personal rapport which existed between Grey and Wilson's special confidant, Colonel House, was also of some assistance to the British cause. But it was Britain's huge war purchases from the United States which offered most protection. Even so a temporary cessation of the German submarine campaign and a redoubled effort by Wilson late in 1916 to bring about a compromise peace reduced Anglo-American relations to their lowest ebb during the war. The Treasury feared that the United States might be in a position to force Britain to make peace in 1917. It was above all the renewal of the German submarine campaign, and the resultant sense of American outrage, which brought the United States into the war in April 1917. Churchill later concluded that American involvement ensured that the war ended in an Allied victory and not – at best – in a stalemate.

Meanwhile much time had to be devoted to the cultivation and conciliation of allies and to the winning of new ones. There was much hard bargaining over territory which had yet to be wrested from the enemy. At the same time the British (and the Dominions) were not backward in taking advantage of opportunities to acquire more territory or regions of influence outside Europe. The empire, formal and informal, was larger than ever by the end of the war, and expansionism and consolidation were deliberately promoted by ardent imperialists such as Lord Milner and Leo Amery partly in the hope that a much strengthened empire would enable Britain to stand aside from future European wars. Amery wrote in 1915:

This war against German domination was only necessary because we had failed to make ourselves sufficiently strong and united as an Empire to be able to afford to disregard the European balance.[43]

Yet this was surely an unrealistic and unwise approach in that, once the balance of power in Europe had been put in jeopardy by the outbreak of war, there could be no going back unless and until the European powers cancelled each other out in such a way that they could pose no real threat to British interests, or unless a substitute could indeed be found for the old power politics. It was an illusion to think that Britain could find the strength, even within an enlarged empire, to distance herself from an unstable and unbalanced Europe. Yet, as we shall see, this mirage continued to fascinate and mislead some politicians – not to mention some historians. As it was, the enlarged empire of 1919 soon proved beyond Britain's means and willpower to sustain in its entirety after the war.

In the autumn of 1918 the Allies were simultaneously confronted by the German acceptance of an armistice, the collapse of the Habsburg and Ottoman empires, and the great question mark which hung over the future of Russia. The victorious powers were not only far from united, but their ability to dictate was much less than in 1814–15, given the strength of popular feeling throughout Europe. Economic dislocation in Central Europe increased the fear of Bolshevism. Thus victory did not provide the victors with a blank sheet of paper on which they were free to draw at their pleasure. Verdicts on the performance of British policy-makers at Versailles have ranged from the highly critical, through suggestions that they did their best in a very difficult situation, to the thesis that – particularly in the case of Lloyd George – there was a bravely imaginative, if finally unsuccessful, attempt to create a just and lasting settlement. The debate turns on the postulated alternatives of a more punitive or a more generous peace; on the degree to which short-term considerations were bound to prevail or were culpably allowed to predominate; on how far historians should concentrate on decision-making at Versailles as opposed to the following years when questions of amendment and enforcement once more arose;

and indeed whether a satisfactory peace was ever more than an idle dream.

Correlli Barnett has no doubts. Versailles was flawed, not because it was too punitive, but because it was insufficiently rigorous. 'If the British had been so minded, Germany could have been divided and permanently weakened in the very springs of power, as the French so desperately wanted.'[44] The possibility of the break-up of Germany in 1919 is effectively disputed by Sally Marks. The British and Americans – governments and peoples – were not willing to intervene in Germany on the scale required. They preferred to hope that the Germans had been taught that aggression did not pay: they exaggerated the finality of the victory. No one, they wanted to believe, having experienced the horrors of such a war, could seriously contemplate its repetition. Nor did they wish to drive Germany into the arms of the Bolsheviks.[45]

The British delegation in Versailles was exposed to conflicting pressures from the start. Domestic demands for the severe punishment of Germany, and for heavy reparations, were soon followed by pressures to cut the size of Britain's armed forces and for a rapid return to normal life. Money, it was argued, ought to be spent on badly needed reform at home rather than on an ambitious foreign policy. Some believed that German reparations would both punish Germany and assist British reconstruction. The desire for revenge, reparations and domestic reconversion to peace, however, revealed a fundamental indifference to the fundamental issue – namely how to provide security for the future. The French were not so short-sighted, though not in agreement among themselves as to how they should proceed. In the end Clemenceau, the French prime minister, insisted that his country would obtain genuine security only through long-term co-operation with Britain and the United States. The harsher the peace the more difficult it would be for France to enlist British and American sympathy and support.[46] As it was the will to enforce even the peace that was agreed withered with alarming speed. Not surprisingly some historians argue that it is difficult to see how, in the atmosphere of 1919 and given the conditions of the time, a better peace could have been negotiated.

Paul Kennedy bleakly concludes that there were 'few simple solutions', and even the finest statesmanship was 'foredoomed, one suspects, to failure given the overall postwar situation'.[47]

Nevertheless both the aims and tactics of Lloyd George remain a matter of contention. Were his day-to-day tactical improvisations truly guided by an underlying strategy, and above all by the assumption that the peace treaty would inevitably be flawed? Was it his prime objective to provide for its revision once passions had cooled and circumstances permitted more rational solutions? Or was there no grand vision? The economist J. M. Keynes as early as 1919 launched the first great assault on Lloyd George's role at Versailles in his famous book, *The Economic Consequences of the Peace*. 'Lloyd George', he wrote, 'is rooted in nothing; he is void and without content; he lives and feeds on his immediate surroundings.' Among present day scholars D. C. Watt, Lorna Jaffe and A. Lentin have all concluded that Lloyd Goerge's prime aim was to win popularity at home.[48] Lorna Jaffe finds ample evidence of self-interest in his famous Fontainebleau memorandum of 25 March 1919 (usually one of the sources most quoted to demonstrate his superior wisdom at Versailles). His plea for a modification of the proposed peace terms to increase their acceptability in Germany was sensible enough in itself, but it was strongly influenced, she argues, by the desire to reduce British commitments as quickly as possible to satisfy the domestic demand for government economy.[49] Lentin is even more outspoken. Lloyd George's delight in improvisation ensured that means began to justify themselves irrespective of the ends. Consequently his 'brilliant "cleverness" . . . fell below the level of events', certainly by comparison with either the 'prophetic vision' of Woodrow Wilson or Clemenceau's tragic vision of 'le monde comme il va'. Lloyd George became too preoccupied with parliamentary success.[50]

These are strong words. Harold Nicolson, though conscious of Lloyd George's domestic calculations, nevertheless commended many of the prime minister's expedients as a skilful attempt to buy time until passions cooled. Nor were they necessarily incompatible with vision or a steady sense of purpose. 'In his [Fontainebleau] memorandum of 25 March, in his great fight of

May 4, he showed that a politician is better when it comes to reasonableness, than a theocrat.'[51] Nicolson was no uncritical admirer – he was after all a disappointed participant at the conference, and as a professional diplomat he was appalled by the many departures from regular and well-proven diplomatic practice. Others have elaborated his argument that Lord George had his eyes both on present political needs and on the process of adjustment over time. They argue that his statecraft must be studied as an entity for the whole period 1919–22. Thus W. N. Medlicott, with his deep knowledge of Gladstone's conception of the Concert of Europe in the early 1880s, suggested that in 'a rather splendid way' Lloyd George was striving to devise a similar instrument with which to tackle Europe's problems. K. O. Morgan is equally insistent that he possessed a 'grand design'. Of all the western leaders he had the boldest and broadest post-war vision to reinforce his spell-binding skills as a negotiator.[52]

According to this thesis Lloyd George believed that domestic and foreign policy were interdependent. Economic recovery and political stability in Europe were essential for the revival of British exports. Employment levels, living standards and therefore social stability at home would all be affected by the level of trade. The punishment of Germany and the isolation of Bolshevik Russia should therefore give way as soon as possible to the restoration of normal relations. From the conference of San Remo in April 1920 to that in Genoa (April 1922), Lloyd George tried to limit the damage being inflicted on the European economy by reparations and other legacies of the war. Late in 1921 he promoted a revision of Germany's frontiers in Upper Silesia at the expense of the Poles. Nor did he forget the need to try to reduce the French sense of insecurity, although the refusal of the United States to join a tripartite security agreement was a sad blow.

To reassure France, appease Germany and reintegrate the USSR into Europe were, in their way, almost as utopian as anything that Woodrow Wilson was trying to achieve, especially when adequate support from home was always in doubt, and when he had virtually no effective allies abroad. Balfour already feared that even the simplest policy – that of trying to contain a resurgent Germany with only France for an ally – might prove too difficult.[53] Morgan concedes that much of Lloyd George's policy was superficially prepared, that he was trying to do too much too quickly, and that he was prone to make promises without looking very closely at the implications. Yet no one tried harder to make water flow uphill: no one showed as much appreciation of the needs of the time. Keynes himself began to acknowledge this as early as 1922, while Lentin moves towards a somewhat similar conclusion once he begins to consider Versailles in the context of its preservation as opposed to its creation. He notes that it was not self-enforcing. What chance, he asks, did Versailles have 'of durability if the victors themselves could not stomach it?' None became more squeamish than the British, and since their conscience could not be wished away, 'it would have been the mark of true *Realpolitik* to take account of it'. This, he concedes, is what Lloyd George tried to do after 1919. Following the latter's fall in 1922, subsequent British governments failed to show a similar sense of urgency and boldness of vision. Although their greatest need in Europe was some sort of equilibrium, they failed to educate the public in the realities of the post-war world. They tended to 'retire and carp at a distance'.[54]

Britain's imperial interests also meant that Europe could not receive her undivided attention. Yet here too British ministers soon discovered the need for selectivity. Thus Curzon's dream of turning Persia into a client state quickly faded. Nationalist forces similarly persuaded the British to settle for more modest roles in Egypt and Iraq. The resurgent Turks also prevailed against the British at Chanak in 1922, a sad climax to one of Lloyd George's more reckless ventures. In a bid to strengthen Greece at the expense of Turkey in Asia Minor, wishful thinking and racial prejudices were allowed to run riot. Straitened resources as well as the gradual triumph of common sense ensured that the policy of 'war imperialism' did not long outlive the war.

Nor did the British gain any benefit from the involvement in the Russian Revolution and subsequent civil war. Once the need to intervene in Russia to oppose the German threat had disappeared with the armistice in November 1918, the cabinet became increasingly divided on policy. Lloyd George was convinced that the internal crisis could only be resolved in the last resort by the Russians themselves. This did not preclude some allied aid to the Whites, partly because of the fear that if the Whites won without British assistance their behaviour would be all the more unpredictable and might even extend to the creation of a new and unholy alliance with a revisionist Germany. Lloyd George, however, had no time for those who argued that Bolshevism had to be destroyed before it began to sow the seeds of revolution within Britain. He insisted that massive intervention in Russia would only intensify discontent at home: he preferred to put his trust in a revival of trade to lessen class conflict at home. Although a later commercial treaty with the USSR failed to live up to his expectations, Lloyd George's instincts were sounder than those of his Conservative critics.[55]

The Great War had discredited the 'old diplomacy' of Salisbury and Grey alike in the eyes of large numbers of people. Even some right-wing politicians and professionals began to look for new ways forward, often because they believed they had no choice if they were to retain or recover public confidence, but also at times because they too believed that something better had to follow so great a blood sacrifice. Even those who recognised that unrealistic hopes were being placed in the efficacy of the League of Nations were so intimidated by the probable effects of another great war upon Britain and her empire that they, in their turn, were inclined to back away from the sort of policies and commitments which might have improved the prospects of a lasting peace. For them it was tempting to hope that leaders in other countries would be equally inhibited, and accept the need for orderly change – if change there had to be. There was an understandable reluctance to run risks or to pile up commitments. Exhortation and negotiation had first to be put to the test.

# 2
# TOO MANY CHALLENGES

THE NAVAL limitation conferences of Washington (1921–2) and
London (1930) stand at either end of a period in which, by and
large, it seemed as if the major states of the world were making
some, if hesitant progress towards the regulation of their rivalries.
There were setbacks, and even at the London conference France
and Italy were unable to resolve their differences. Many outstand-
ing questions still menaced Franco-German relations, and of
many of the accords concluded in these years it soon became
evident, as A. J. P. Taylor has remarked, that the promises were
'black and big on paper, and only there'.[1] Nevertheless British
policy-makers had sundry, if short-sighted reasons for experien-
cing a sense of modest satisfaction. Britain's relations with
France, the United States and Japan on the whole were turning
out to be less disturbed than had seemed possible at the beginning
of the 1920s. Some progress was made with the problem of
Germany, while Bolshevism was proving only an embarrassment,
not a major threat outside the territories of the USSR. The ten-
year rule, whereby the British services were instructed to plan
on the assumption that they would have ten years notice of a
major war, was being automatically renewed each year. Churchill
as chancellor of the exchequer in the middle of the decade fought
against the naval estimates as tenaciously as he had fought
for their increase before 1914. Ministers, preoccupied by the
problems of war debts, by the difficulties experienced by the
British economy in a vastly changed world, by the rising

expectations of large sections of the population, as well as by the grievances of the unemployed and poor, preferred not to encumber themselves with an expensive foreign policy.

Fears of serious unrest at home and of an electoral backlash if popular expectations were not fulfilled were a major influence on ministerial thinking in these years. Here was a major explanation for the readiness of Conservative leaders such as Austen Chamberlain and Balfour to persevere with Lloyd George's wartime coalition after 1918. Neville Chamberlain at the start of the 1924 ministry insisted that 'unless we leave our mark as social reformers, the country will take it out of us hereafter'.[2] Apart from electoral and other domestic consider-ations, informed opinion was much more strongly in favour of what the *Manchester Guardian* of 31 January 1924 described as 'The New Diplomacy' compared with the period before 1914. Lowes Dickinson, in his *International Anarchy* (1926), articulated the widespread desire for a permanent escape from the secret diplomacy and the alliances and ententes which were held responsible for the war of 1914. Exponents of *realpolitik* were muted in public, though Balfour privately asked, *à propos* of the ten-year rule, whether one could guarantee peace so far into the future. The Conservative leader, Stanley Baldwin, in 1930 did not exclude the possibility of another war in the distant future, and warned that military weakness could diminish the nation's freedom of choice as it became more dependent upon others for security. There was a warning from the Imperial General Staff in 1923 that the 'Great War' should not be regarded as 'exceptional, but the greatest lesson we have ever had,' while Austen Chamberlain, soon after his appointment as foreign secretary in 1924, brooded over possible threats from the USSR and, within a generation or so, from Germany unless she became prosperous and reconciled to a constricted but tolerable existence in Europe.[3]

In the 1920s a sense of potential British vulnerability therefore co-existed with the desire, even the determination to believe that affairs were moving in the right direction, and that radical new initiatives were unnecessary. On the one hand a Foreign Office memorandum in 1926 set out the possible dangers even if Britain herself took a non-aggressive course. 'The fact is that war and rumours of war, quarrels and friction, in any corner of the world spell loss and harm to British commercial and financial interests.' In contrast a memorandum on Anglo-Soviet relations after Locarno oozed complacency from every sentence.

> Having virtually reassumed the diplomatic leadership of Europe, she [Britain] can afford the luxury of individual restraint, where others, less reflective and less interested, are not afraid to tread. She can, in fact, bear the privilege of independence without the odium of isolation.[4]

Increasingly in the 1920s it was the more complacent perception which became most widespread in British governing circles.

The United States was an early source of embarrassment, especially for those who had hoped that the First World War would lead to longer term Anglo-American co-operation. Not only did the United States fail to join the League, but differences with Britain over war debts, naval, commercial and other rivalries threatened to push the two countries further apart. British efforts to reduce these causes of friction have not found universal favour among historians. Although W. N. Medlicott accepts that the Washington Treaties of 1921–2 conferred some benefits upon Britain, he nevertheless insists that the British government 'must be criticised for its willingness to secure the immediate emotional satisfaction of a dramatic act of friendship and temporary pacification at the cost of a permanent weakening of the British position in the Far East'. Maurice Cowling is more caustic. Britain sold the pass to Japan in 1922 when she chose subservience to the United States rather than renew the Anglo-Japanese alliance. For Correlli Barnett, Washington was one of 'the major catastrophes of English history, . . . which was to exercise a cumulative and decisive effect on the future of English power'. The British, by ending the Japanese alliance, helped to strengthen those in Japan who wished to follow more chauvinistic and aggressive policies. Ties with Japan were weakened with no compensating tightening of relations with the United States. Washington was an 'act of faith' like the ten-year rule.[5]

There are two prime questions to be considered here. Could the British have taken any other decision in 1921–2? Might a continuation of the alliance have given the British more security in the Far East in the 1930s? Ian Nish, in the most notable study of the decline of the Anglo-Japanese alliance, agrees with Sir Charles Eliot, the British ambassador in Tokyo at the time. The latter considered the alliance 'really dead before its termination' at Washington in 1921–2.[6] Although the rise of Bolshevism in Russia supplied a common threat of sorts, the British were becoming more conscious of Japan as a trade rival – and perhaps something more ominous – in China and yet further afield. Might Japan develop into a Far Eastern Prussia? Could she become the leader of a Pan Asian movement whose influence might spread as far as India?[7] Had the time come to try to find an alternative to the Anglo-Japanese alliance, or was that the only instrument open to the British through which they might hope to exercise a restraining influence on Japanese ambitions?

Fortunately for the British there were powerful forces at work in the United States which favoured naval limitation. Moderate groups were also in the ascendant in Japan which were willing to make concessions to reduce the arms burdens on the Japanese economy and in general to seek more cost-effective methods of promoting national interests in the Far East than had recently been the case. In short, negotiations from the summer of 1921 were facilitated by a growing willingness in all three capitals to explore ways to reduce friction. At the same time it must be conceded that this, the first major example of arms limitation, was a largely self-interested cost-cutting exercise. On the insistence of the Americans there were no commitments to ensure future respect for the treaties – other than a promise to consult in an emergency. Nevertheless a foundation had been laid for further negotiations to regulate both naval rivalries and the conduct of the relations of the three powers with each other in the western Pacific and with China. Overall the 'Washington system', at the time of its creation, appeared to be a constructive and forward-looking act, and one which stood out in contrast both to pre-war diplomacy and to the disappointments attendant upon Versailles. Nor was it possible in the early 1920s to anticipate the Great Depression, its effects upon a country such as Japan, or the failure of other powers to respond to renewed Japanese militancy.

The early 1920s in Europe were dominated by the German question and the French occupation of the Ruhr. Britain had only limited leverage at this time, and immediately following the fall of Lloyd George the nation had little taste for an innovative foreign policy. The economic consequences of the French occupation of the Ruhr, however, were serious enough to prompt action by the United States as well as by Britain, and the succeeding Dawes (1924) and Young (1929) plans gave the impression that the problem of German reparations was being managed if not solved. In the absence of deeper American involvement second or third best schemes were welcome. Additional (if what once again proved to be insubstantial) comfort was drawn from the Locarno agreements of October 1925. These provided a collective guarantee of the French and Belgian frontiers with Germany, while Germany herself was admitted to the League the following year. Similar progress was not possible in Eastern Europe where Germany would not accept that the frontiers had been fixed for all time, and where the British had no intention of entering into any commitments. Furthermore even in Western Europe no military plans or preparations were made by Britain to implement their promises. Sir Austen Chamberlain, the British foreign secretary, resembled a spent force after his efforts at Locarno. Overall he was satisfied with a semi-detached relationship with Europe, qualified only by a tendency to lean towards France and to grumble over German ingratitude and demands for further revisions of the Versailles treaty.

Not surprisingly historians apply such descriptions as 'limited detente' or 'a respite of civility' to this period. British policy was selfish and blind, if 'encased in elevated rhetoric'. But account must also be taken of the widespread post-war fatigue and disillusionment. An alliance with France to contain Germany was unthinkable to most people: indeed many thought France greatly to blame for the continuing sense of grievance in Germany. Few accepted the degree to which British security was still bound up with stability in Europe. The service chiefs were usually more interested in the defence of the empire than in preparing for further action in Europe. Thus neither the option of standing firmly beside France to demonstrate that the Versailles territorial settlement was sacrosanct, nor that of offering modest concessions to meet some of Germany's more reasonable complaints (in the hope of consolidating the German 'moderates' in power) was seriously considered. But one can fairly observe that if the hands of the policy-makers were tied, they themselves showed no great eagerness to untie them. Only at the end of the decade, when time was running out, were there reviving signs of alarm within some of the departments in Whitehall.[8]

Britain's international position began to deteriorate rapidly in the early 1930s. By March 1932 Japan's military actions in Manchuria and Shanghai had persuaded the Committee of Imperial Defence that it was imperative to relax some of the restraints upon British defence expenditure. Within two years, following the rise of Hitler, Germany was displacing Japan as the main potential threat. Yet warnings that war might come as early as 1939, coupled with the collapse of most disarmament talks by 1934, failed to inspire a sufficient sense of urgency. Neville Chamberlain as chancellor of the exchequer advocated a new understanding with Japan in the Far East in order to concentrate on rearmament against Germany in Europe. In particular he hoped that a larger air force would not only provide security against Germany, but would equip Britain with the leverage needed to persuade Berlin to conclude a general European settlement on a basis of genuine give and take. Yet occasionally even Chamberlain's optimism and patience wore thin. 'If only', he complained in March 1936, reflecting on the cost of rearmament, 'it wasn't for Germany we would be having such a wonderful time just now' with the British economy. 'What a frightful bill do we owe to Master Hitler, damn him!'[9]

The Foreign Office did not share Chamberlain's belief that an expansionist Japan could be conciliated. It also feared that attempts to do so would antagonise the United States. True, it shared in the widespread exasperation with the American fondness for words without action in the Far East, yet key officials accepted that in the long run Japan could not be stopped without

American assistance. The situation deteriorated further in 1937 when a full-scale war developed between Japan and China, only for the Foreign Office to discover at a conference in Brussels in November 1937 that the United States was still unwilling to make a stand. From the British chiefs of staff came further warnings that they lacked the forces with which to risk war in Europe and the Far East simultaneously. There was nothing for it but to try to defend British interests against Japan with such diplomatic tools as were available, while taking note of any American hints which suggested that in time something more substantial than anti-Japanese rhetoric might be forthcoming. On the whole historians have been reasonably satisfied with the conduct of British policy towards Japan in these years. Indeed, had Germany not won such spectacular victories in Western Europe in 1940, Britain and the United States might ultimately have been able to devise a credible strategy of deterrence in the Far East. In due course Japan might have been persuaded that she had no rational choice but to return to something akin to the 'Washington system' of the 1920s.

Meanwhile fear of Japan in the 1930s had some, if not a decisive influence on British policy in Europe. When Britain tried to bring pressure to bear on Mussolini during his bid to conquer Abyssinia in 1935–6, the Admiralty took fright, not because it did not expect to win a war against Italy, but because it believed the loss of some major units of the fleet would aggravate its already difficult, if not impossible task in the Far East. Fear of Japan also helps to explain the eagerness with which Britain agreed to the Anglo-German naval treaty of 1935, a treaty which it was hoped would restrict the German fleet to little more than one-third that of Britain. Much more than in the period before 1914 the British, in the late 1930s, were conscious that they did not have enough navy to go round. Navalists found one scapegoat in the Washington and London treaties, yet these were symptoms rather than causes of British vulnerability.

It is much more difficult to decide whether British policy-makers were indeed presented in 1935, as many writers have claimed, with an indisputable opportunity to halt the advance of the revisionist powers before their momentum became too great. Once it became apparent that Mussolini was determined to wage a major war of conquest against Abyssinia, the British government faced a difficult choice. Such a war would pose a direct challenge to the League of Nations at a time when, partly because of the Peace Ballot (an ambitious survey of public attitudes on Collective Security), the League was attracting great popular attention in Britain. The decision later in 1935 to hold a general election also meant that the government could not afford to allow the opposition parties to become the sole champions of collective security. On the other hand British interests in Abyssinia were insignificant; Germany and Japan posed much more serious threats; France was still hopeful of reaching a military understanding with Italy which might be of use against Germany. Indeed, had the French cabinet been united in its refusal to support the League, the British government would have had a reasonable excuse for inaction. As it was the cabinet was tempted to follow a twin-track policy, trying on the one hand to persuade Mussolini to accept a compromise over his demands in Abyssinia, while at the same time trying through support of the League to exert limited yet sufficient pressure to compel him to be reasonable.

Mussolini, however, was not to be bought off or intimidated. War in Abyssinia followed. Early in December 1935, with the British general election safely over, the cabinet authorised the foreign secretary, Sir Samuel Hoare, and Vansittart to sound out the French premier, Pierre Laval, on the next move. Vansittart (the permanent under-secretary in the Foreign Office), driven by his fear of and his desire to oppose Germany, took a leading part in the formulation of a bold offer to conciliate the Duce. Unfortunately more was agreed more quickly in Paris than the cabinet had anticipated and, worse, news of the Hoare–Laval pact soon leaked out. There was a great public outcry in Britain, though it is possible that the cabinet was even more impressed by criticism from backbench Conservative MPs who insisted that so blatant a departure from collective security was impossible after the declarations they had made in support of the League in the recent election campaign. Baldwin bowed to the storm. The pact was still-born, and Hoare was replaced as foreign secretary. Yet in the end, and despite not a little diplomatic activity in the first half of 1936, the cabinet finally accepted Neville Chamberlain's argument that Mussolini's victory in Abyssinia was a *fait accompli*. To persist with half-hearted sanctions was 'the very midsummer of madness'.

On the whole British policy in this unhappy episode has found few defenders, especially given the belief that the imposition of oil sanctions might have forced Mussolini to give way before the League had to resort to force. Although the case for the Hoare–Laval Pact is based on the argument that Germany and Japan posed more serious threats to British interests, critics see the whole Abyssinian affair as a mortal blow to the League and an encouragement to aggression elsewhere.[10] Hitler, for instance, decided to advance the remilitarisation of the Rhine by a year. Yet in the end it perhaps did not matter so very much either way. Hitler would have continued his search for openings, and unlike Mussolini he had a powerful and purposeful nation at his back. In September 1939 he still chose war although Mussolini refused to fight. On the other hand Britain and France were unlikely to achieve any lasting success in their efforts to conciliate Mussolini unless Hitler was permanently tethered.

Meanwhile, with varying degrees of optimism and pessimism early in 1936, the Foreign Office was working on plans for a comprehensive settlement with Germany. But Hitler took everyone by surprise with his remilitarisation of the Rhineland in March 1936, and, worse, deprived Eden (the British foreign secretary) of what he had hoped would prove a useful bargaining counter. Even so Eden still assured the House of Commons on 18 June 1936 that the government's aim was 'nothing less . . . than a European settlement and appeasement'. The pace of rearmament remained modest, and there was little enthusiasm for closer ties with France. Baldwin continued to fear that a military defeat of Germany would open the door to communism, while France's recently negotiated pact with the USSR was an object of suspicion – in part because it seemed likely to entail deeper French involvement in Eastern

Europe.[11] Soviet participation in the Spanish Civil War from the autumn of 1936 confirmed the fears in London.

There was a rather greater sense of urgency in 1937 as German armaments continued to increase, and the British economy suffered new setbacks. It seemed improbable that crises over the future of Austria and of the large German population in Czechoslovakia could be long delayed. In any case the new prime minister, Neville Chamberlain, was by temperament driven to approach policy-making more purposefully and impatiently than Baldwin, and he easily persuaded himself that any delay might make the situation in Europe yet more explosive. He refused to believe that any general settlement with Germany was likely to prove an illusion.

But this eagerness to reach such a settlement became a matter of intense national controversy from 1938, a controversy which shows few signs of diminishing 50 years later. D. C. Watt has dismissed most accounts of British foreign policy in the era of appeasement written before the 1960s as 'emotional, guilt-ridden and politically inspired'. The opening of the archives and the passage of time, however, have not significantly tempered the debate, although its character has changed in a number of respects. The vast extent of the documentation, official and private, has made an overall mastery of the subject increasingly difficult. Indeed Paul Kennedy has complained that some scholars, half-buried in the voluminous primary sources, have thought it sufficient to lump together all the conceivable reasons for the policy of appeasement. No one, he observes, has yet developed a 'grand theory' to explain appeasement,[12] a failure which some historians will doubtless view with relief. A. J. P. Taylor has added a warning of his own – namely that ministers may often have decided policy first and then looked for reasons to justify it.

One fruitful line of inquiry relating to appeasement has been the exploration of its more deeply rooted origins. As early as 1952 Arnold Toynbee suggested that the British had become 'prematurely humanized' in their approach to foreign affairs. The idea was elaborated by F. S. Northedge who demanded an analysis of the 'whole [British] mental approach to foreign relations'. He went on: 'it is evident how ill-adapted were the entire style and temper of British foreign policy to the international relations' of the 1930s. This was largely because of 'the force of certain widely diffused moral and political ideas, pacifist, humanist, bourgeois and eminently unfanatical, rather than in calculated disloyalty to democratic ideals on one side of the political fence or confused Socialist or internationalist notions on the other.' It was to these that Taylor was referring when he described Munich as, in a way, 'a triumph of all that was best and enlightened in British life'.[13] Martin Gilbert goes so far as to describe Chamberlain's policy as an 'honourable quest', while Sir Michael Howard concludes that the MacDonald and Baldwin governments gave 'an anxious attention to electoral moods which would have gladdened the heart of E. D. Morel and his colleagues in the Union of Democratic Control; moods which they personally profoundly shared'.[14]

The continuity in style and thought processes of British politicians and diplomats from the Victorian era has often been emphasised. Correlli Barnett, for instance, attributes these to the peculiar educational and social environment in which the post-Palmerstonian elite grew up. Kennedy stresses the persisting 'aristocratic detachment, the tendency to understatement and irony, the appeal to reasoned argument'. Above all there existed a faith in compromise, and a lack of insight into the driving forces in the expansionist states of the twentieth century.[15] It is also true that British politicians were adept at clothing mundane and selfish considerations in fine language. Indeed British self-interest and idealism interacted to such effect over a long period that the influence of the former over the latter was easily forgotten. When everything seemed to lead to a certain decision it was often impossible even for the person who made 'the decision to know what was . . . the most important factor in it'.[16] British success over the years could still lead to periods of self-confidence and to a predisposition to expect other peoples to share (or in time to be persuaded to share) the same assumptions. F. S. Northedge commented on the frequent failure to perceive that 'politics are not everywhere run by men whose footrule is the profit and loss account'. Yet at the same time there existed among the British leadership a very real awareness of Britain's growing vulnerability in the world, and Kennedy writes with unnecessary diffidence when he asks whether the pleas in favour of moderation were not a sign of something deeper – 'an uneasy apprehension of future national decline and a private sense that the country had passed its peak'.[17] These fears were very real and influential.

This sense of weakness helped to determine policy in advance and was not simply trotted out as an *ex post facto* rationalisation for what had been decided. As early as 1924 Admiral Beatty was warning that Britain's eastern empire was dependent upon Japanese self-restraint or American assistance. When Japan cut loose in the early 1930s Vansittart was soon arguing that Britain could escape disaster in a war in the east only with American assistance. But at the same time even those ministers who were prepared to acknowledge that the world might not yet be ready for arms limitation and the triumph of reason over ambition feared that extensive British rearmament would alienate the electorate once living standards were put at risk. Labour would gain at the polls from Conservative efforts to stand firm abroad. Baldwin, Halifax and Chamberlain have all left evidence of their sensitivity to the demands of *innenpolitik*. Hankey complained bitterly as early as 1931 that British power abroad since 1919 had been sacrificed to social reform and other domestic extravagances. British pacifism, in his opinion, owed less to idealism than to exhaustion, economic weakness and domestic priorities.[18]

Bernard Porter reviews the alternative policies which might, in theory, have been open to Britain. These were an essentially isolationist policy based upon the empire, collective security, European integration as mooted by Aristide Briand of France in 1929, a comprehensive understanding with Germany, or abdication as a world power. He concludes that none was 'remotely realistic'. Vested interests, national prejudices and material constraints forced Britain to seek short-term profit or security at the expense of 'future ruin'; she had to follow her traditional interests in an accommodating spirit as cheaply as possible – hoping all the while that the worst would not happen. Or as Kennedy puts it:

> it may help us to understand better the overall context of British policy in the inter-war years if we bear in mind that these are the actions of a country with nothing to gain, and much to lose, by being involved in war. Peace, in such circumstances, was the greatest of national interests.

Appeasement could seem 'natural', war was irrational for a nation overcommitted abroad and with pressing domestic calls upon its resources.[19]

Not all scholars, however, are persuaded that, after due allowance has been made for the above constraints, one need stop there. Account should also be taken of the problems faced by Britain's opponents and of those occasions when the British might safely have encouraged stronger action by, for instance, France; have responded more positively to overtures from the USSR; or have shown more enterprise in their courtship of the United States. Appeasement in their view was a disastrous choice in that at best it was resented as unwarranted interference by the German leaders and at worst was despised for its weakness. In other words, many continue to support Churchill's argument that this was an unnecessary war in that decisive action at the appropriate time might well have frustrated Nazi ambitions. Through the succesful containment of Germany the British would have lessened the capacity of Fascist Italy to make mischief – and very possibly Japan would have confined her military operations to China. Such a policy, it is contended, would not necessarily have strengthened the USSR significantly or increased British dependence upon the United States (two outcomes much feared by Chamberlain). Had war been avoided a balance of power might have been created in both Europe and the Far East which was less damaging to British interests than the sequence of events which actually unfolded between 1938 and 1945. Detailed examination of what options were open to Britain in 1938 and 1939, why the leadership acted as it did, and of the wisdom of British policy-making is thus still necessary. Not all choices in 1938–9 had necessarily been pre-empted by the constraints set out earlier.

In the debate for and against appeasement scholars have been compelled to examine not only British policy-making in minute detail, but that in other capitals as well – in Paris, Berlin, Moscow, Washington, Tokyo and Rome as well as in London. Unfortunately the intentions of other governments are also the subjects of on-going controversy and remain so whether there is (as in the case of Germany) or there is not (as in the case of the USSR) an abundance of archival evidence.

It has taken many years for historians to come properly to terms with even some of the more obvious constraints guiding policy in Britain. Thus until the 1970s there was no detailed study of the economic and financial obstacles to rearmament as perceived by the Treasury. There is now reason to suppose that even a hypothetical British cabinet which was inspired to oppose Nazi Germany would have been impressed, if not wholly daunted, by the unpalatable implications of an expensive rearmament programme. More than unimaginative Treasury parsimony was at work. Even the limited scale of rearmament which was undertaken from the mid-1930s soon ran into shortages of machine tools and skilled labour. Up to one-sixth of the relatively modest 1937 arms programme had to be met from imports. Fears of balance of payments problems soon developed, with the British economy lacking the strength and versatility (as well as the opportunities) to boost exports quickly. Rearmament also revived memories of wartime inflation and consequential labour unrest. The electoral implications could not be ignored.[20] Nor in the later 1930s could the British look automatically to the United States for economic assistance in the event of war, given the strength of isolationist feeling in that country and the passage of the Neutrality Legislation. Admittedly Chamberlain and other leading figures had no wish to become dependent upon the United States. American help, if it were forthcoming, would be at the price of more than British pride. Nevertheless the Treasury had to acknowledge early in 1939 that Britain's economic problems in the event of war would soon become acute without American assistance. The scale of British economic weakness is now increasingly acknowledged even by critics of appeasement, if only with the result that they argue that a weak hand was played with 'crass ineptitude'.

It does not, however, necessarily follow that British policy would have been much more assertive given a stronger economic base at home. This is highlighted by the subjective manner in which information from Germany was so often analysed. Recent research has demonstrated both how badly informed the British were concerning German preparations for war, and to what selective uses the available intelligence was put. Anti-Soviet preoccupations and prejudices in British Intelligence worked to the advantage of Nazi Germany. At first British Intelligence was too weak and uncritical to measure or comprehend Nazi rearmament. Improvements in the mid-1930s were offset by a predisposition to believe that German preparations must be as defensive in motivation as those undertaken in Britain. Arms limitation agreements still seemed to offer hope for the future. Only in the autumn of 1936 was there serious alarm about the extent of Nazi aims and capabilities, and thenceforward British Intelligence either exaggerated German military power or evaluated it uncritically, giving little or no attention to weaknesses of which Germany's own military leaders were only too conscious. Unwarranted assumptions were made about totalitarian efficiency and clarity of purpose. The degree to which Hitler relied on bluff, intuition and improvisation was not consistently appreciated.

Hence some scholars remain convinced that a more objectively advised and differently motivated British cabinet might have chosen other courses of action, especially in September 1938 when no assessment was made of the longer term strategic implications of the abandonment of Czechoslovakia.[21] They note the failure of the chiefs of staff in September 1938 to modify their advice to the cabinet (that is, to avoid war until 1939 at the earliest) despite their dawning realisation that south-east England was unlikely to suffer a 'knock-out blow' from German bombers at the start of a war. True, a reassessment of the German air threat by the British, even in 1938, would not have altered the situation on land where the British were dependent upon the French. The latter were totally unprepared (not least psychologically) for offensive action, while the relationship between the governments and the military chiefs of the two countries was profoundly unsatisfactory. Marshal Weygand later described such military understandings as existed between Britain and France as 'merely the sickly heir of twenty years of mutual suspicion and hesitation'. A stronger stance by both powers in 1938 would have required a relationship of much greater confidence and intimacy built up over a number of years. Nor can it be argued that the British were the sole cause of the ultra-cautious policies followed by the French from 1936. From the Rhineland to Munich French passivity was at least as much the result of national choice as of British pressure. Furthermore, without an earlier change in British defence policy, war in 1938 would have left any serious fighting (for six months or more) to France and Czechoslovakia. Others would have been called upon to make the first real blood sacrifice.

Nor did the policy of appeasement mean that Chamberlain was simply a milksop politician. He handled opponents at home with great firmness – just as he dealt with French efforts to wring more binding commitments from him. He also approached the German question with strong convictions. Indeed their very strength was a weakness. Information was selected and interpreted to support his preconceptions. Even if the Allied military position had been stronger his overall aims would have been similar, though his tactics might have differed. Above all Chamberlain wanted a comprehensive settlement with Germany. Perfect all-round justice was impossible in Central Europe. The weaker peoples had to bow to the stronger, but the stronger for their part had to demonstrate that their aims were limited, their methods in pursuit of revision reasonable, and their long-term commitment to peace, arms limitation and international co-operation genuine. A reduction in the political tensions in Central Europe was also expected to make for improved economic conditions, in part but not solely as a result of the reduction in defence expenditure. Even some measure of preferment for German trade and economic influence in parts of Eastern Europe might have been acceptable. German prosperity, according to conventional British economic theory, was expected ultimately to add to the welfare of others. Unfortunately it became all too easy for Chamberlain to make more and more concessions as he pursued the mirage of a satiated Germany. Concessions which seemed a small price to pay for peace among the powers were in fact being made for worthless promises.

Although Chamberlain admitted to occasional fears concerning the apparent irrationality and unreliability of the regime in Berlin, his whole being recoiled at the horrendous implications if such should be accepted as the truth. Thus passing thoughts on the possibility that Hitler was 'half-mad' only added to his urgent desire to take no risks – it would be all too easy to blunder into an accidental war by trying to put pressure on so unstable a personality. Chamberlain and his strongest supporters had therefore to be absolutely convinced that Germany's aims were indeed unlimited and that no compromise was possible before they revised their policy. In the summer of 1938, for instance, his foreign secretary, Lord Halifax, could not persuade himself that general war in Europe was conceivable simply over the question of the future of the Germans living in the Sudetenland in Czechoslovakia. Even if Germany were defeated he professed to believe that a just peace would still reduce the territorial extent of Czechoslovakia – it was beyond his imaginative powers to anticipate the forced movement of populations which was to follow the defeat of Germany in 1945. Nevertheless Halifax proved more sensitive than Chamberlain at the height of the Sudeten crisis in September 1938. Briefly he saw Hitler's demands and conduct as so outrageous that they were beginning to transcend what were ostensibly the central issues. It was no longer simply a crisis over the future of the Sudetenland. Towards the end of September, therefore, the British appeared to be steeling themselves for war – that is until the eleventh hour when Hitler himself hesitated. The Munich conference thus became possible at which, although Hitler later seemed to regard it as a defeat, the German dictator secured the Sudetenland and Czechoslovakia's fortified frontier in return for cosmetic and nebulous promises of good conduct in the future. In such circumstances Halifax could not bring himself to share Chamberlain's satisfaction, only his relief that war had been averted.

At a time when the sounding of public opinion was in its infancy, the degree to which Chamberlain's policy was supported in the country at large cannot be established with any precision. Halifax himself wrote in some alarm to Chamberlain on 23 September 1938, when Hitler's demands at Godesburg outstripped those submitted at Berchtesgaden a week earlier, and when the prime minister showed signs of yielding yet again. Halifax warned that the 'great mass of opinion seems to be hardening in [the] sense of feeling that we have gone to [the] limit of concession'.[22] There is evidence of such a trend from other sources. Yet the sense of relief which followed Munich was widespread and genuine, even if only a minority viewed the agreement with any degree of contentment or genuine confidence concerning the future. Criticisms by the Labour Party during and after the crisis sprang from deep feelings, but at the same time most historians doubt if the party possessed a realistic alternative strategy. Though Labour's front bench on big occasions in the Commons could sometimes put together a presentable case, the party in practice remained divided and uncertain on foreign policy whatever the degree of unity engendered by its deep hostility to Chamberlain.[23]

Apart from the widespread desire for peace there were many in Britain who asked what would be the cost and consequences of a war even if the nation were ultimately victorious. Britain's wealth would be diminished – at home and abroad. High taxation, increased government control of the economy, a probable advance of socialism and egalitarianism, greater domestic tensions and discontents had all to be anticipated. A war-devastated Europe would be a fertile breeding ground for communism, and the balance of power would be shifted strongly if not decisively in favour of the USSR. The USSR and communism might also make gains outside Europe, not least at the expense of the British Empire. Japan and the United States were other likely beneficiaries. The remedy could be worse than the disease – indeed it was tempting to insist that the remedy would be much worse as long as the worst case against the Nazis was deemed non-proven. Thus Chamberlain and his admirers did not have to be pro-Nazi, or aspire to introduce into Britain the 'gentlemanly' form of Fascism which some of their critics on the left feared was their objective. A defence of the status quo at home and abroad provided them with ample grounds – in their eyes – for trying to avert a European war.

Scholars who argue that Britain could and should have run more risks in the autumn of 1938 may well be right – in the abstract. Yet often they too are able only to highlight why the British leadership acted, and was in general allowed to act as it did. They may even unintentionally reinforce the arguments of those, such as the distinguished German historian, Klaus Hildebrand, who argue that it would have been surprising had Britain, given her past experience and her current circumstances, followed a different policy in 1938.[24] Chamberlain spoke from the heart as well as from self-interest when he insisted to the American ambassador on 21 September 1938: 'war is the end of this civilization – that Communism or something worse is liable to follow'. The same fears can be encountered in many quarters. Even Churchill asked in 1937 if victory would feel very different from defeat.[25]

For a time after Munich Halifax and Cadogan, the permanent under-secretary in the Foreign Office, seemed to resolve Britain's customarily ambiguous policy towards Central and Eastern Europe (an aversion to commitment counter-balanced by a reluctance to give Germany a totally free hand) by resigning themselves to German preponderance. As Cadogan wrote, 'let Germany, if she can, find there her "lebensraum" '. Britain should content herself with influence in those states which flanked the eastern Mediterranean and the Middle East, areas of prime interest to the British Empire.[26] Halifax also looked to the empire and even the United States to redress the balance as Germany extended her influence. But such hints of British disengagement from Central and Eastern Europe naturally continue to excite those who are in search of evidence that Chamberlain's government deliberately encouraged Hitler to advance eastward and into conflict with the USSR. This, they claim, was the prime purpose behind Munich. The 'Guilty Men' approach is very evident in a fairly recent Soviet study of Russian foreign policy.[27] Published Soviet documentation is full of contemporary Russian suspicion of the Chamberlain ministry.

That Chamberlain and most Conservatives entertained a deep distrust of and hostility towards the USSR is not in dispute. Baldwin had declared earlier that it would not break his heart if Hitler and Stalin came to blows, and had warned Eden not to allow Britain to be dragged into war on the side of communism. Eden's distrust of the USSR was apparent in 1937.[28] Even after Munich Lord Perth, the British ambassador in Rome, could intervene in a debate among British diplomats on the relative significance of National Socialism and Communism (in so far as they affected British interests) with the observation that, while the threat from the former might be 'more immediate, that of communism, though remoter, is more wide-reaching and insidious'. The Nazis might aspire to world domination, but communists, by their very philosophy, had to work for the destruction of the British Empire and capitalism.[29] Even more 'incriminating', at first sight, is a remark attributed to Chamberlain in December 1938 that he thought Hitler most likely to drive eastward, 'in which case we might well not be involved at all'.[30] Yet within a month Chamberlain, while visiting Mussolini in Rome, thought fit to warn the Duce, when the latter spoke of a probable German–Polish or Russo-German war, that while 'such a war would not necessarily involve the Western powers also, . . . once war began one never could tell when or where it would stop'.[31]

In practice, however, even when calculations based on self-interest pointed to a reappraisal of British policy towards the USSR, the British could not rid themselves of the belief that the Soviets were looking for and hoping to exploit a German war with the Western powers. Soviet enthusiasm for collective security in the mid-1930s had to be weighed against their professed belief in the inevitability of war between the capitalist powers. For what it was worth, a Russian defector in 1937 had insisted that Stalin was interested in a deal with Hitler at the very time when the USSR was ostensibly and ostentatiously giving priority to the pursuit of collective security in the person of its foreign minister, Litvinov.[32] German documents also suggest that some approaches were made before Munich. It is true that the most thorough Western study of Soviet foreign policy in these years argues that, until Munich, the British might have been able to negotiate an understanding of some sort. It was Munich, according to Haslam, which 'opened the fortified gates of Eastern Europe to German tanks, . . . and also left Litvinov struggling to preserve the few bare threads of the policy he had so painstakingly pursued'. The Soviet leaders were disorientated by Munich: the isolationists in the Kremlin were strengthened. Haslam himself, however, admits his dependence on documentation from the Soviet foreign ministry and its embassies abroad, so that Stalin's own thinking remains very much a matter of guesswork.[33]

There was a time when Hitler's occupation of Prague in March 1939, the disruption of Czechoslovakia and his blatant repudiation of Munich were widely regarded as a turning-point in British foreign policy. This interpretation is now seen to belittle the impact of a number of strange but alarming rumours and other developments upon British policy-makers from the winter of 1938–9.[34] Halifax and others had already begun to have second thoughts about giving Germany broadly a free hand in Eastern Europe. Even Chamberlain had written, rather pathetically, on 11 December 1938, 'it would be a tragic blunder [by Germany] to mistake our love of peace and our faculty for compromise, for weakness'. Most alarming to the British government were the reports that Germany might, early in 1939, be about to strike westward – perhaps against the Netherlands, Switzerland, or possibly even in the form of a surprise bombing assault on London itself. Worrying, too, was the apparent growth of a fatalistic mood in France. Fears in London that France might be losing the will to resist Germany produced new promises of support in February, and these were soon followed by the first tentative steps towards the creation of a sizeable army to fight on the continent, a radical change in British defence policy. The Treasury now found itself isolated when it protested against the cost of yet more arms increases. Halifax replied that risks had to be run with the British economy in the knowledge that the economic strain 'could not last indefinitely'. Germany's economic problems would soon force her leaders to choose between war and the probability of an internal crisis. Britain had to arm to deter Germany and, if necessary, to fight.[35]

Chamberlain's confidence, however, soon returned. When no German aggression occurred, and with Britain's air defences improving, he was to be found writing egotistically to his sister as early as 19 February: 'I think they [the dictators] have had good cause to ask for consideration of their grievances, and if they had asked nicely [sic] after I appeared on the scene they might already have got some satisfaction.' He was still hopeful as late as 23 and 30 July that Western strength would finally persuade Germany that negotiation was the only sensible option. In the meantime Britian had to avoid the provocative approach recommended by Churchill.[36] Not even the German occupation of Prague in the middle of March 1939 provoked an immediate protest from Chamberlain. This hesitation has led to suggestions that only concern at the outcry in Parliament and among the public persuaded him to protest against German conduct. According to David Carlton,[37] some senior Conservatives feared a party split headed by Eden to form a coalition with Labour and the Liberals. Maurice Cowling detects the hand of Halifax – 'the embodiment of Conservative wisdom who decided that Hitler must be obstructed because Labour could not otherwise be resisted'. But by this time there were those in the Foreign Office who were anxious to initiate a stronger policy, and they too contributed to the decision to offer Poland a guarantee at the end of the month.[38] Activists were assisted by rumours that Germany was about to deliver an ultimatum to Romania, and by the fear late in March that Poland might make terms with Germany unless Britain and France came to her support.[39] The decision to give the guarantee was taken in haste in Britain and with inadequate reflection upon its many implications.

The chiefs of staff were much more conscious than the politicians and the diplomats of the difficulty of honouring the guarantee to Poland. If they were now more confident that Germany could not inflict a knock-out blow from the air against Britain, they knew that even with French help they could not prevent a German conquest of Poland. Not a few historians have followed Churchill and Liddell Hart (the leading contemporary military writer) in criticising the decision to offer the guarantee. Churchill in *The Gathering Storm* thought that, whereas it would have made sense to fight for Czechoslovakia in 1938, in March 1939 Britain accepted the risk of war 'on far worse conditions' for a state which had joined in the assault on the Czechs six months earlier. The decision had been taken 'at the worst possible time and on the least satisfactory ground'.[40] The action has been described more recently as a 'remarkable' act, forced on the government by parliamentary criticism. A 'blank cheque' was given to 'notorious' practitioners of 'reckless diplomacy' in defiance of the policies followed since 1919.[41] Careful military calculations certainly did not guide the cabinet and Foreign Office: there existed only a greater feeling of security against German air attacks on Britain. The main imperative was the fear of losing the political initiative yet again. Berlin had to be persuaded that in any future negotiations pre-emptive German moves would not be tolerated. In so far as thought was given to the military implications, it was hoped that the threat of a two-front war would either deter Germany or, failing that, would ensure that an eastern front would increase the economic pressure on Germany, and at the very least would buy time for the Western powers.

Obviously this sort of military calculation does not stand up to close examination, especially in the light of what followed. But one must not ignore the contemporary belief that something had to be seen to be done (for foreign as well as domestic reasons), nor the persisting hope of Chamberlain in particular that war was not inevitable. It was, in his mind, still a question of discovering the right mix of diplomacy and strength to persuade Hitler to negotiate honestly and constructively. He still hoped that Hitler would prove amenable to reason, even if Britain now threatened with the stick as well as continuing to proffer the carrot. The guarantee in any case applied only to Polish independence, not to the maintenance of the existing status quo in Eastern Europe in every detail. The future of the city of Danzig, for instance, was thought to be negotiable. Germany, however, was still expected to contribute to a general European settlement.

Any verdict on the guarantee must also be influenced by one's perception of German intentions. Britain (and France) by accident may have committed no error in giving the guarantee if one accepts the thesis that Hitler, either through a settlement with or by the defeat of Poland, was simply clearing the way for an early onslaught in the west.[42] The guarantee might not have achieved the intended Anglo-French object, but it could have been a step in the right direction had it been followed by a determined bid to ally with the USSR. A much more effective two-front deterrent or instrument for war might then have been built up against Nazi Germany. On the other hand it can be argued that nothing should be regarded as inevitable, and that whatever the outcome of Hitler's dealings with Poland, a German assault in the west was not the inevitable sequel. Germany, the USSR and the Poles would all have faced very different scenarios. In particular there might have been less scope and, on the German side, no incentive to negotiate with the USSR. As it was the Polish guarantee, in the short run, was mainly of benefit to the USSR – despite Moscow's initial suspicion. In practice Stalin was soon exploiting the new openings to negotiate with Germany and the Western powers.

A recent Soviet study of inter-war foreign affairs has confidently asserted that Chamberlain was forced to negotiate with the USSR by an outraged British public at a time when he was still intent on a deal with Germany. The USSR would have preferred a deal with the Western powers, but in the end was driven to conclude the pact with Germany because of Western equivocation, delay and general lack of seriousness. Yet despite reference to an impressive amount of documentation this Soviet work makes no mention of a discreet approach to Berlin as early as 17 April 1939, three days after a British overture in Moscow asking for a public promise of Soviet support for any neighbouring state under threat from Germany. Other German documentation which highlights the ensuing Soviet approaches – admittedly often indirect and circumspect, but cumulatively significant – is ignored. Only on 20 August, it is argued, did the Soviets reluctantly decide that they could not do business with the British.[43] On the basis of all the available evidence it is not unreasonable to argue that the Soviets, rather than simply and assiduously courting the British and French, were sensibly keeping their options open in Europe. The British negotiators, though very conscious of the restrictions under which they were operating as a result of the anti-Soviet prejudices of Chamberlain and many others in London, often believed that their Soviet counterparts were deliberately drawing out the negotiations and introducing new demands just when progress was apparently being made on one issue. Historians who imagine, or who claim, that all that was required was good will and drive on the part of the Western negotiators underestimate the psychological and material obstacles to an agreement which existed on both sides. These are fully illustrated by the dispatches of both foreign services, British and Russian.[44] Nor could the British easily ignore the resolute opposition of the Poles to any co-operation with the USSR.

Thus it simply was not possible for either side to concentrate upon what should have been their main concern – namely the German threat to all and sundry. Each side wanted to be sure that any concerted action was compatible with their needs as perceived at the time. To the British it seemed on occasion that they were being asked to concede, at least potentially, to the USSR the very hegemony which they were trying to deny to Germany in Eastern Europe by co-operation with the USSR. Had the British been truly ruthless they might have concluded that a deal with Russia was their best hope, in that whatever happened in Eastern Europe, Russia and Germany would have been brought into direct opposition to each other. This was precisely what Moscow feared, and the Russians negotiated accordingly. The Soviets also had good cause to reason that even if they placed the most generous intepretation on British thinking (which obviously they did not), and the Western powers honoured their guarantee to Poland, the poor state of Western military preparedness and planning meant that the initial burden of any war would still fall on Russia and Poland. Once Hitler was prepared to make what was ostensibly a generous offer to Stalin concerning the partition of Poland and the apportionment of influence in Eastern Europe, only the conviction either that

Hitler was not to be trusted or that concerted action by Britain, France and Russia would prevent war in Eastern Europe might have persuaded Stalin that a deal with the Western powers was the wiser choice. As it was, in August 1939, he was sufficiently confident that Hitler would not extend his quarrel with Poland to a war with the USSR to decide that a bird in the hand was worth two seemingly immobile birds comfortably nesting behind the Maginot Line and the English Channel.

It was widely suspected at the beginning of September, and still is by some historians, that Chamberlain would have avoided war if he could even after German forces began their unmistakable advance into Poland. Certainly his critics in Parliament and in his own cabinet hastened the declaration of war as Chamberlain, for as long as he dared, clung to the hope that Hitler was not in fact trying to destroy Poland as an independent state. Halifax, too, was anxious to explore every avenue until persuaded that war was the only option.[45] When or whether they would have finally declared war in the absence of strong pressure from ministerial colleagues and from Parliament is not something that can be established with absolute certainty, though a case can be made on the basis of their earlier thinking that their ultimate concern was always an outcome which would place some restrictions on German growth and ambition. In the end a variety of developments at home and abroad rather than their own precise calculations determined that the independence of Poland would be the test case.

Furthermore the partially fortuitous nature of the stand on behalf of Poland helps to explain why some historians continue to question whether this was the correct issue on which to opt for war even in September 1939 – despite Hitler's record. Thus Maurice Cowling, while refusing to devote time to might-have-beens, insists that the 'curious thinking', which was much influenced by 'the shadow of "British democracy"' and which lay behind the decisions of March and September 1939, must be laid bare. There is the need, he insists, to examine 'the assumption that it was neither morally obligatory nor pruden-tially self-evident that Hitler should be obstructed in Eastern Europe'. Roy Douglas is more direct, and complains that emotion exerted too much influence on British policy at this time. He detects 'a large element of what we might call the heroic – or the irrational' at work in Britain as well as in Germany.[46] Indeed he contends that Chamberlain should be criticised not for his policy of appeasement but for his failure to stand by it to the bitter end. In his view Britain's one chance of escaping from decline as a world power lay in the development of her empire and the avoidance of war if at all possible.

But matters had surely gone too far by September 1939, and such arguments also assume greater far-sightedness, greater freedom of choice, and greater control over affairs than politicians can customarily expect to enjoy. After all, Hitler himself would have preferred to delay the war in the west. At the same time it is evident that the British had stumbled into war without a careful calculation of the strategic realities. In so far as there had been a policy, it had been primarily diplomatic, and it had failed in its objectives – with respect to both the USSR and Nazi Germany. Militarily the British were in the remarkable position that the Treasury believed that the nation could afford only a short war whereas the chiefs of staff calculated that it could win only a long one.[47] Thus P. M. H. Bell suggests that it is easier to see why the British government was so averse to war in 1938 for military reasons than why it went to war in 1939 'with a modest confidence' in victory.[48] Again one notes Chamberlain's optimism, reluctant belligerent though he was. He believed that Germany could not inflict a knock-out blow against Britain and France, and he drew comfort from the calculation that economic warfare in particular might yet bring Germany to her senses. If it was no longer possible to put any trust in Hitler, Chamberlain still hoped that enough Germans would favour compromise once they realised the full implications of an all-out war – especially one which they could not expect to win. The spectacular German successes of 1940 were not foreseen.

Indeed the scale of the German military victories in Scandinavia, the Low Countries and above all in France in the spring and early summer of 1940 was such that even Chamberlain's successor as prime minister, Winston Churchill, experienced occasional private doubts as to whether Britain could realistically continue the fight. The escape from Dunkirk was a sort of victory in that it sustained British morale at a critical moment. For some, notably King George VI, the release from continental entanglements was almost a bonus. A prolongation of the struggle did not seem entirely pointless, if only in the hope that Germany might concede better terms. Ultimate American help was a possibility. The situation was desperate but not quite hopeless, and those ministers who had contemplated negotiations with Berlin via Rome were persuaded to soldier on for the time being.

Fortunately, too, Germany was not properly equipped to carry the war across the Channel. Major tactical mistakes were made in the handling of the Luftwaffe during the Battle of Britain, so that in the face of the remarkable efforts of Fighter Command Germany lost her one chance of victory in 1940. The Italian entry into the war seemed almost an advantage in that British successes in that theatre were good for the national ego. Japan, too, was content for the time being to push no further than northern Indo-China. The Japanese, anxious to put an end to outside aid to the Chinese Nationalists, were unable to persuade the British to close the Burma Road for more than three months. On the other hand Britain's international financial situation was deteriorating rapidly, and could be remedied only by trans-Atlantic assistance. Similarly it would only be a matter of time before the German submarine directly threatened Britain's survival. To a degree unknown in modern times Britain's future lay in the hands of leaders of other powers, both friendly and hostile. Britain's chosen stance in 1940 was truly heroic. It was also, fortunately, more heroic than many of her people appreciated at the time.

# 3

# FROM WORLD WAR TO COLD WAR

MANY BUT not all the disasters which a major war was expected to inflict upon Britain and her empire duly occurred in the 1940s. Territory lost to Japan was recovered, even if the movement to independence in the Indian subcontinent, Ceylon and Burma was accelerated. At home a Labour government from 1945 proved less radical in its policies than expected. Austerity, admittedly, was more rigorous than during the war, and internationally Britain seemed destined to stagger from economic crisis to economic crisis. Yet within ten years of the defeat of Germany expectations of improving living standards for most people were rising as never before. As anticipated the USSR and communism were making great advances, while the United States was now the pre-eminent liberal capitalist power. But all Europe did not succumb to communism, and the British could often find comfort in the thought that they were the most important and influential of America's allies. The war itself had been a harsh and punishing experience, but it had been less demoralising than that of 1914–18. Even the Cold War brought its compensations. It led to American aid to facilitate the economic recovery of Western Europe. Heavy expenditure on armaments helped to sustain the post-war boom. The Cold War ensured the division of Germany, a cause of many serious problems though of a lesser magnitude than those occasioned by that country earlier in the century. Finally the Cold War contributed to the development of a more than customary degree of co-operation among the West Europeans.

Not surprisingly, therefore, British foreign policy came to be widely regarded as something of a success story in the period down to 1955, especially in comparison with the 1930s and even the 1920s. Britain, it seemed, though the least of the 'Big Three', had succeeded in occupying the common ground of three interlocking circles as defined by Winston Churchill – the United States, the Commonwealth and Europe. The lessons of the 1930s had seemingly been learned. More than at any time since the 1890s Britain appeared to be striking the right balance between guns and butter, firmness and conciliation, independence and association with others. Naturally there were dissenting interpretations, but these attracted only marginal attention until the changed circumstances and perspectives from the 1960s. The opening of the archives also enabled historians to develop more critical insights into policy-making. Only then were such issues as Britain's own contribution to the onset of the Cold War, the wisdom of her stand-offish policy towards post-war Western Europe, her extra-European activities, and the adverse consequences of her close relationship with the United States widely debated. Churchill and Ernest Bevin (the formidable foreign secretary in Attlee's Labour government from 1945 to 1951) no longer towered quite so impressively over their predecessors.

Britain had had no prospect of victory over Germany until the forced entry of the USSR and the United States into the war in 1941. Yet their entry also meant that achievement and exploitation of victory would be primarily a Soviet-American affair. As early as 1942 earnest discussions took place in the Foreign Office on Britain's post-war prospects. Some younger officials, impressed by the decline of British power and the growing calls upon limited resources, raised the possibility of 'handing over the torch' to the United States and the USSR. Such ideas were emphatically rejected by their seniors: they feared that the nation's fate would be delivered into the hands of Russia, the United States or even of a revived Germany if Britain deliberately chose second-class status.[1] The usual Foreign Office assumption was that Britain must be one – if only the third – of the leading powers. There existed, as Victor Rothwell notes, a deep 'psychological impulse' to remain a great power'.[2] Officials were already troubled by the extent of Britain's wartime dependence upon the United States. The Americans were already trying to put a ceiling on Britain's gold and dollar reserves, and were thus threatening the prospective influence of sterling as a post-war international currency. American ideas on post-war international trade, with their emphasis on multilaterialism, appeared to threaten imperial preference. Similarly American interest in international trusteeships to replace colonial regimes menaced the empire itself. The defeat of the Axis, it seemed, might simply prove the prelude to a non-military assault upon many of the foundations of British greatness – the City of London, the Sterling Area, and the varied resources which the British drew from the empire.

Yet while Churchill might grumble that he had not become the King's first minister to preside over the liquidation of the British Empire, he more than any minister was a positive – even a romantic – advocate of the closest possible post-war co-operation with the United States. Others took a more pragmatic view of the future. The chancellor of the exchequer warned in April 1944 that it would be 'impossible to maintain Sterling [after the war] without some assistance from the United States'. It was conceded by the Foreign Office that if the United States were asked to 'underwrite the Empire, they would expect some say in its running'. Indeed, the Foreign Office – more optimistic than the Colonial and India Offices – began to argue that America's bark might prove worse than its bite. There was yet time – while the war made it impolitic for the United States to press its case to the full – for the British to educate their American colleagues in the realities of the Sterling Area, imperial preference and colonial rule as understood by the British. They might appeal to the less dogmatic of the American leaders and work upon their desire for orderly post-war development. Roosevelt, though often impulsive and radical in conversation, was a gradualist in practice, more interested in progress in the right direction than in immediate results.

The extent and character of Soviet influence in the post-war world similarly excited apprehensive speculation. But there was steady movement from the view expressed as late as November 1941 that, 'ideologically, we are as far removed from the Soviet as from the Nazi regime: they are both hideous tyrannies'.[3] Gradually the debate edged forward from whether the Russians were Bolsheviks or barbarians to the possibility that their conduct might become more acceptable and they themselves more open to reason. It seemed possible that the leaders in the Kremlin might be losing their revolutionary and ideological obsessions to become practitioners of conventional power politics; that they might be evolving into a people with whom one could do business. Admittedly Russian secrecy was a persistent barrier to understanding, and more pessimistic assessments were also possible. Perhaps the Russians would not advance far enough beyond their 1941 frontiers to play their full part in the defeat of Nazi Germany. Alternatively, and more often, it was feared that they might advance too far into the heart of Europe bearing the germs of communism with them. Lord Ismay confessed that after three visits to Moscow he was no nearer an understanding of the Russian mentality than before.[4]

Given the limited information on Soviet policy-making scholars have ample room in which to use their imagination. There are broadly three main schools of thought on British (or Anglo-American) policy towards the USSR during the war. At one pole stand those who argue that, for various reasons, opportunities were missed to win the confidence of the Soviet leaders by honest and generous diplomacy. Such critics are sometimes in danger of attributing to Stalin and his colleagues a sensitivity they did not possess. At the other extreme are those who argue that the Western leaders, including Churchill, failed to take a sufficiently strong stand against Stalin's wartime demands, especially on Poland, and thereby encouraged the Kremlin to become even more exacting. Moscow was tempted to extend Russian influence into Eastern Europe in the expectation that the Western powers would – at worst – protest to satisfy their own publics. In between are those who argue that wartime relations should not be seen in such black and white terms; that in practice there was give and take on both sides; and that until the defeat of

Germany East–West relations were not fatally compromised by any wartime decisions. A further variant, that by and large the British took a more realistic view of Soviet ambitions than did the Americans, has been increasingly questioned in recent years.

Amid these controversies it is possible to detect some convergence, namely the realisation that British perceptions of and policies toward the USSR between 1941 and 1945 were far from consistent, and that, whether scholars incline to the view that policy was on the whole too hostile or too conciliatory, in neither case was there a comprehensively developed and applied strategy. Hence Vojtek Mastny's complaint that British policy was 'undistinguished', while Martin Kitchen argues that Churchill's reactions to the USSR were 'often impulsive and inconsistent'.[5] In practice, however, decisions relating to the USSR – from the question of a Second Front (that is, an Anglo-American invasion of northern France) in 1942 or 1943 to that of the western frontiers of the USSR – could rarely be considered simply on their merits by the British leadership. Thus Churchill, during his last year in office, often seemed anxious to take a stronger stand against the USSR. Yet in practice Britain was too dependent upon the United States to act on her own – except in Greece. Furthermore it appeared by no means certain in 1944–5 that the German threat was being eliminated for all time. Some in the Foreign Office thought Russian domination in Eastern Europe preferable to that by Germany. Finally, in 1945, there was still a war to be won in the Far East.

Various instances can be cited of the desire in some quarters to reassure the USSR. Indeed a number of efforts to avoid offence were perhaps carried to excess. Thus a veto was imposed on the interception and decoding of wireless traffic from the Soviet embassy in London.[6] Wishful thinking in high places, up to and often including the prime minister, cannot be ignored. Long years of habit and experience, based both upon national interest and weaknesses, had made the search for accommodation almost instinctive in the Foreign Office. Here too could be found the feeling that the Second World War should not be automatically treated as the prelude to another great confrontation. There was the further hard-headed calculation that the USSR at the end of the war would be too well-entrenched in much of Eastern and even Central Europe for its authority to be directly challenged. Doubts concerning the extent of post-war American involvement in Europe similarly meant that the British could not lightly afford to offend the USSR.

Yet some scholars continue to insist that opportunities were missed to strengthen the Anglo-American position in Europe. Much turns here on one's assessment of the character of the Soviet leadership, and how it would have responded to tougher bargaining during the war years and how far it would have honoured any ensuing agreements. Stalin's record of extreme ruthlessness balanced by cautious opportunism provides no certain answer. The moderate peace treaty with Finland and his acquiescent response to British intervention in Greece are not proof that more assertive and co-ordinated Anglo-American diplomacy in Eastern Europe would have made much difference in the long run – assuredly in the absence of strong physical pressure. Furthermore even attempts at far-sighted planning could easily have contrary results. This is well illustrated in the case of Italy. Here, in the preparation of Allied control machinery, the Foreign Office initially considered a system which would have provided for true three-power co-operation and which might also have created a basis – however fragile – for later Anglo-American claims to an effective say in the political future of states in Eastern Europe, the Soviet military monopoly notwithstanding. In practice the exclusive manner in which the British and Americans exercised control in Italy from 1943 was later used as a precedent by the Russians for their own methods of control in Eastern Europe.[7]

The difficulties of foreseeing the consequence of diplomatic decisions are well illustrated by the outcome of the wartime plans for the temporary division of Germany into three occupation zones, largely on the basis of British proposals drawn up in 1943. The permanent division of Germany – and certainly not its division into the East and West Germanies which finally emerged – was not anticipated or desired by British planners. They devised what then seemed an adequate interim scheme to avoid inter-Allied disputes and to administer Germany after its defeat. It was also hoped that three-power co-operation here might prove a basis for co-operation elsewhere. Soviet fear of Germany was acute. Given security there, with Russia's western borders agreed and acknowledged, and its status as one of the Big Three confirmed, leading British figures hoped that satisfactory longer term relations might be established with Moscow.

Thus the Foreign Office was shocked by suggestions from the British chiefs of staff in the middle of 1944 that resources in those parts of Germany under post-war Western control might be needed at some future date to help stem the advance of the USSR. Only later did it agree that contingency plans should be prepared, and then in the utmost secrecy.[8] Meanwhile optimists in the Foreign Office were encouraged by reports from the British embassy in Moscow in 1944 and even 1945. The Russians were portrayed as sensitive, suspicious and fearful, as well as arrogant, clumsy and ambitious. It was condescendingly suggested on 27 March 1945 that Russia would slowly 'emerge from her [boisterous] puppydom and settle down to the serious and respectable business of collaboration with her major allies', particularly the British if the latter displayed the right mixture of firmness and understanding. The Russians might be unpredictable and opportunistic, but basically they were realists who respected realism in others. They would be particularly tempted to do business on the basis of spheres of influence. The more sceptical in London, meanwhile, could always reflect that British public opinion was as yet unprepared for a rift with the USSR, and if and when it occurred it was important to demonstrate that the fault did not lie in London.[9]

In Poland the British could hope to exert little or no direct influence, although Churchill did his best to persuade the Polish government-in-exile in London to reach a compromise with Stalin. He hoped the latter might be satisfied with the movement of Poland bodily westward at the expense of Germany, and with a friendly, but freely elected government. Unfortunately Poland was the high-road between Germany and the USSR, and the British interpretation of what would satisfy the Kremlin far exceeded what the Poles were willing to concede and fell even further below what Stalin decided were his needs.[10] The British entertained higher hopes of influence in parts of South-Eastern Europe, but detailed examination of British wartime strategy reveals that they were less obsessed with this region and with anticipating the advance of the USSR there than has often been claimed. Churchill's efforts to limit post-war Soviet influence date largely from the spring of 1944. Foreign Office interest throughout the war in the encouragement of Balkan and even Eastern European federations sprang from the hope that these might lead to greater political and economic stability and progress, and lessen the risk of excessive interference from *any* neighbouring great power. In 1944 there were more serious and specific British efforts to limit Soviet influence in the Balkans, but only in Greece did the British have the opportunity to act to any effect.[11]

Nevertheless even at the end of the war in Europe the British were still hesitating over the appropriate course of action. They were unsure how much support they would receive or indeed wanted to receive from the United States. They continued to entertain hopes of tolerable relations with the USSR. Ideally in tackling the problem of Germany they required the constructive support of both the superpowers. If the American commitment was unpredictable, satisfactory relations with the USSR were all the more important. The extent of Anglo-American differences is well illustrated by some of the briefing papers prepared by the State Department for the Potsdam Conference in July 1945. These stressed the danger that Britain might try to draw the United States into her quarrels with the USSR. Far better that the United States should mediate between the two. In practice the Americans had their own differences with the USSR, but just as Roosevelt in his wartime meetings with Stalin had been careful on many issues to distance himself from Churchill, so Truman and his secretary of state, Jimmy Byrnes, at first largely went their own way in dealings with the Russians. Even British help in the war against Japan was received with mixed feelings, and if the United States was less active in favour of decolonisation than had been expected, the Anglo-American intimacy of the war years was rapidly disappearing. With the cessation of Lend-Lease after the defeat of Japan in August 1945, Britain was for the moment seen in the guise of a suppliant rather than as a necessary ally. John Maynard Keynes, Britain's leading economist who was sent to Washington in search of financial aid to speed Britain's post-war economic recovery, quickly discovered that Americans were not impressed by the argument that Britain – in return for her extraordinary war effort, and in particular for fighting alone in 1940–1 – had a moral entitlement to American economic assistance. For the time being Britain's best claim to American economic aid was the realisation by experts in Washington that their aspiration to create an open, multilateral world economy would thrive only with British assistance – given the international role of sterling and the extent of the empire. Britain had to be helped back on to her feet if she was to co-operate.

Pro-American leanings in any case were far from universal in Britain in 1945. Disillusionment with the USSR was only just beginning. Many Labour critics of Soviet methods at home and abroad could still feel that communism was less aggressive than American capitalism. Some in the Labour Party entertained serious hopes of the introduction of a distinctively 'socialist' foreign policy, while within the government itself there existed at least a readiness to review the 'conventional wisdom of diplomatic orthodoxy'. Attlee's cabinet was more inclined to consider alternatives than would have been the case had Churchill been victorious, although with Ernest Bevin as foreign secretary there was no question of following the more radical ideas of certain left-wing intellectuals. Bevin defended British interests robustly against all comers. Thus he was soon complaining that the Monroe Doctrine was being extended to the Far East and he was wary of American economic leverage whether it was used to promote liberal multilateral trade or protectionism. In his turn he shocked some Americans with his readiness to use the language of traditional power politics. Early collisions with the USSR led Stalin to complain that Bevin was no gentleman. Yet his combative approach did not mean that Bevin despaired of co-existing with Russia from the outset. He also tried to modify traditional British policies in the Middle East and to pay more attention to the wishes and interests of the local peoples. Bevin was not merely a 'Lord Palmerston in a cloth cap' as one of his critics later wittily remarked. Nor did he ignore the United Nations.[12] At the same time it was only during his first year in office that Bevin began to grasp the full extent of Britain's post-war problems. But he refused to panic, and it was the pressure of circumstances, not some predetermined strategy on his part, that led to the revival of the wartime intimacy with Washington.[13]

The new prime minister, Clement Attlee, for a time seemed eager to embark upon an open-minded reappraisal of British foreign policy. He was even willing to examine how far Britain's straitened economic circumstances and her over-extended position in the world might be eased by new forms of international co-operation. He asked, for instance, whether some international agency might replace the existing British military presence beside the Suez Canal and guarantee freedom of passage.[14] Others in his party went further in principled objection to many of Britain's worldwide activities. There was also support in various quarters – from sections of the Labour Party to the Foreign Office itself – for some sort of Western European third force. Britain, it was suggested by some professional diplomats, would fare better as the leader of such a grouping than as the very junior partner in an alignment with the United States. Bevin himself hoped that in time such a third force would acquire significant economic bargaining power in the world. These were attractive projections, but it was difficult to transform them into something substantial. The French, the essential partner, had ideas and interests of their own, and were especially difficult to deal with as long as General de Gaulle was in power. Communist strength in France became another worry, with civil war at times seeming possible. Only at the end of 1947 was Bevin reassured by the firmness of the French government's opposition to communist-inspired strikes and riots, and only then did the permanent exclusion of communists from office seem assured. In any case by the winter of 1947–8 Bevin was beginning to think increasingly in Atlanticist terms, especially as it became apparent that the post-war economic problems of Britain and Western Europe were unlikely to be solved in the foreseeable future without substantial American assistance.

Meanwhile in 1945–6 consciousness of Britain's post-war economic vulnerability – she was now the world's greatest debtor – failed to produce dramatic changes in British foreign policy. Even a Labour government proceeded cautiously.[15] It was axiomatic in the Foreign and Colonial Offices and the defence departments that Britain should remain a world power, and few politicians were in fundamental disagreement with that objective. There was thus no delay in the reoccupation of the territories lost during the great Japanese offensives in 1941–2, and some attempt was also made to rebuild Britain's financial and commercial influence in China in the face of American competition and Chinese obstructionism. The early indepen-dence of India was anticipated, but the defence planners still hoped that Indian forces would make a major contribution to the defence of the Commonwealth in Asia. Diplomats and service chiefs pressed ahead with the maintenance of British political and military influence in the Middle East, and in general were able to limit the influence of those ministers who questioned the ability of Britain to support so expensive a commitment.

American Lend–Lease ended in August 1945. It was already evident that Britain would be unable to pay her way in the world for several years. An American loan seemed to many the easiest way to limit the discomfort during the period of transition. But both on the left and right stood critics who insisted that alternative options existed, and that American money would be forthcoming only on unacceptable terms. The cabinet itself agonised over acceptance when it was presented with the American terms. In the end ministers were swayed by the fear that without the loan their domestic reform programme would suffer, and by the electoral damage they would suffer from continuing and even intensified austerity.[16] Keynes himself was more impressed by the international arguments. In 1944, although the Americans held most of the financial cards, he had been deeply involved in the Bretton Woods conference which fathered such institutions as the International Monetary Fund and the World Bank. These were designed to encourage multilateral trade and international economic growth after the war. Keynes feared a return to the autarkic tendencies of the interwar years unless Britain and the United States were able to co-operate. Failure might also strengthen isolationism in the United States. True there was a heavy price to be paid for the loan – notably the convertibility of sterling in 1947 – but he was convinced that the British themselves would suffer in the long run if they looked primarily to the Sterling Area and to the Commonwealth for markets and imports, and if they failed to support those in the United States who favoured multilateralism.

Keynes also saw the loan in the context of Britain's continuing role as a world power. Early in 1946 he argued that it was 'primarily required to meet the political and military expenditure overseas. . . . The main consequence of the failure of the loan must, therefore, be a large-scale withdrawal on our part from international responsibilities.' In addition to the occupation forces in ex-enemy states and the usual imperial garrisons, British forces were deployed for a time in Greece, Indo-China and the Dutch East Indies. Manpower tied up in the armed forces added to the labour shortages at home. There were other costs such as the need to supply food to the British occupation zone in Germany. These calls upon the nation's resources have only recently begun to receive the detailed attention they deserve, but they form an essential part of the wider debate on the wisdom of British policy decisions taken immediately after the war. On the one hand so many foreign commitments undoubtedly increased the difficulty of converting the economy from war to peace, and absorbed resources which could have been otherwise employed. Had it not been for the American loan a comprehensive reappraisal of Britain's foreign commitments must surely have taken place. In its absence much was therefore decided which helped to shape British foreign policy over the next twenty years. As it happened, in the course of time, the costs of these commitments became rather more bearable, but Britain was still saddled with heavier defence burdens than most of her leading industrial rivals. On the other hand those in authority – and many historians have subsequently agreed with their judgment –

anticipated possible communist gains or regional chaos if the British indulged in precipitate and ill-considered withdrawals.[17] Furthermore the British in practice (though often not from deliberate intent) were buying time while the Americans began both to accustom themselves to their new role as a world power and to establish their priorities. The British, indeed, were much swayed by instinct, tradition and special interests. Yet it would have been remarkable had they foreseen the pace of the post-war retreat of the old imperial powers from Africa and Asia. George Orwell, for instance, in his striking work, *1984*, assumed that the greatest powers would continue to manipulate large areas of the globe with relative ease. For the British government to have embarked upon a policy of precipitate withdrawal in the later 1940s would have been widely regarded as defeatist and as a premature act of abdication entailing prospective material as well as immediate political loss.

Nevertheless contemporary and later debate on British policy in the Middle East deserves further consideration. Thus Phillip Darby asks why, once the independence of India was accepted, and given the upsurge of new political forces in the Middle East, Britain failed to see that it was time to go. The prime minister himself pushed hard for a truly radical review of British foreign and defence policy in this region. Lord Bullock comments on one of the papers submitted by Attlee, that of 5 January 1947, that here was 'perhaps the most striking sketch of an alternative foreign policy' to be devised after the war.[18] The 'perhaps' may seem redundant, but it may be justified by the fact that Attlee had himself put a question mark against his own ideas a year earlier. He had then remarked that all might seem very different if the United States became seriously interested in this region. Nevertheless in the intervening months Attlee subjected both the Foreign Office and the defence chiefs to a barrage of perceptive and searching questions concerning the wisdom and viability of their current policies and recommendations for the future. On the surface he appears to have had much in common with left-wing critics of British 'imperialism' in the Middle East. In practice his arguments were much more down to earth.[19] Did it make sense, he asked, in the light of Britain's ailing economy, the development of new weapons, the overwhelming conventional strength of the USSR compared with what Britain could muster in the Middle East, and the danger that the USSR might be provoked rather than deterred, to persevere with a military presence in Greece, Palestine, Libya, Iraq and in Egypt? He suggested a retreat to a line across the centre of Africa, remoteness from Soviet sources of strength being the best defence of British interests; a redeployment which would still protect a route to the East, that through the Mediterranean being unusable in the event of war.

Yet his abandonment of this plea for a thorough review of British strategy was as dramatic as the line of argument itself. The reason for his retreat is far from clear. Montgomery claimed that he had led the service chiefs in a combined resignation threat early in 1947 unless Britain continued to hold the Middle East, an assertion which has apparently been confirmed by no other source.[20] More significant, probably, was the evolution of the thinking of Attlee and a few chosen colleagues on nuclear weapons. By January 1947 they had decided to press ahead with the development of a British bomb. Furthermore the chiefs of staff had produced a comprehensive statement on defence which persuaded Attlee that they were at last facing facts in a rapidly changing world. The defence chiefs set out the revolutionary implications for Britain of the dawning nuclear era. The nation, they argued, would prove so vulnerable that war would scarcely be a usable instrument of policy. Deterrence would become the best form of defence. Since, in the event of a European war, Soviet conventional strength would – in the foreseeable future – overrun most of non-communist Europe, the USSR would have to be deterred by nuclear armed bombers flying from secure bases within reach of Russia's key political and industrial centres. This meant bases in Britain and in the Middle East so that key targets in both northern and southern Russia would lie within range. That Britain would not possess the means to strike at the USSR with nuclear weapons for at least ten years was deemed irrelevant. A major war with Russia was not considered probable within that period. What mattered was that Britain should still have the requisite Middle Eastern bases if ever the scenario outlined above became a reality.

The summer of 1947 found Attlee backing Bevin in support of a continuing British presence in the Middle East against critics in the Labour Party, and despite the protests of his chancellor of the exchequer at the scale of overall British defence spending.[21] Not even the economic crisis in the summer of 1947 could shake the resolve of Attlee and Bevin. Middle Eastern oil was paid for in sterling (not the rapidly evaporating dollars). There were also the repatriated profits from British oil companies in Iran and elsewhere. All contributed to the nation's purse, so that Bevin could indeed argue that his Middle Eastern policies were helping to defend the living standards of the British working man. If the British withdrew there was no guarantee, it was said, that the Middle Eastern states would act responsibly, while the dangers of Soviet penetration would increase. British interests could not be left to chance, or as Denis Healey wrote in *Cards on the Table* (1947) for the edification of the public and the Labour Party, any reduction in Britain's foreign commitments 'must be carried out in an orderly way so that at no point do we lose our power of initiative and our ability to control the process'. There must be no power vacuums: these would only result in fresh conflicts as new powers intruded. In August 1949 Bevin kept up the pressure in the cabinet by insisting that the Middle East, on account of oil and its strategic location, ranked second only to the United Kingdom itself in the scale of Britain's foreign priorities.

The determination of the British to stay had also been reinforced by the knowledge from 1947 that Washington wished them to do so, and that at some stage in the future American assistance might be forthcoming. This was part of the gradual convergence in Anglo-American diplomatic and strategic thinking from 1946. While the refusal of the United States to continue the wartime collaboration in the development of nuclear weapons, the terms of the loan, and the public and often acrimonious differences over the future of the Jews in Palestine, received and continue to receive much attention, on a number of issues discreet co-operation and an awareness of common interests were steadily developing. Admittedly it was a less tidy experience than the traditional story might suggest. The chapters on the re-creation of the wartime special relationship, from Churchill's speech at Fulton to the British contributions to the introduction of the Truman Doctrine, the development both of Marshall Aid and Nato, all prove on closer inspection to have been less straightforward than as set out in the original version. The British were not simply engaged in a far-sighted holding action and educative exercise until Washington woke up to post-war realities.

Both governments were greatly influenced by the course of events. Various options were explored. Bevin's vehemence in Anglo-Russian negotiations did not mean that he wholly despaired of some sort of *modus vivendi*. Some who worked closely with him believed that he did not move consistently against the USSR until after the failure of the foreign ministers' conference in London in November–December 1947. Bevin unfortunately left relatively little on paper so that his conduct is often open to more than one construction. But he wrote revealingly on 18 June 1946:

> We should not ourselves work for a breakdown of the Potsdam Agreement or for the splitting of Germany along the border of the Russian zone. If there has to be breakdown the responsibility must be placed squarely on the Russians.[22]

In various ways he tried to keep the door open for further talks with the USSR and to minimise any impression that the British and Americans were acting in concert. Yet Bevin also wanted American involvement in Europe, particularly in Germany. As he told the cabinet on 3 February 1947, he did not want the future supervision of Germany to be left to Britain, France and the USSR alone. The Americans should also play their part.[23]

Progress towards closer Anglo-American co-operation did not arise simply in response to problems relating to the heart of Europe. Much occurred as a result of the identification of common interests on the periphery of Europe, in the Mediterranean and the Middle East. Eisenhower as the American army's chief of staff remarked in February 1946 that in many matters relating to the armed forces, military equipment and intelligence, the two countries were so bound together that some forms of collaboration had to continue, however informally.[24] In that year, with the formation of the American Strategic Air Command, the potential value to the United States of air bases in Britain against the assumed enemy, the USSR, was recognised. A year later the Americans began to see similar hypothetical attractions in air bases in Egypt from which to strike at southern Russia. Sites in Western Europe were not considered at this time, mainly because in the event of an East–West war no land-based defence was in prospect against the numerous conventional forces of the USSR. The loss of most of Western Europe at the start of a war was therefore assumed. The counter-stroke would have to be launched by Britain and the United States from the periphery. Wartime Anglo-American associations and memories facilitated inter-service communication – communications which were often kept secret from the politicians, or of which the politicians preferred to remain in official ignorance. Yet at the same time the British Air Staff could fret over their dependence on the United States, especially given the determined efforts of the latter to preserve its nuclear monopoly. They continued to plan for the day when Britain's own nuclear force would provide bargaining power in Washington as well as serve as a deterrent against the USSR. Included in Bevin's arguments for a British nuclear force was the political leverage he expected it to confer upon a British foreign secretary when negotiating with the Americans.

Meanwhile the British welcomed growing American interest in the fate of Iran, Turkey and Greece in 1946 – the Soviets were looking for gains both in Iran and Turkey, while civil war raged in Greece between the communists and the seriously divided parties of the centre and right. But the British were careful not to commit themselves too obviously. Fears of American inconstancy were still strong. It is also doubtful if the British engineered an American commitment in Greece and Turkey in quite so calculated a manner as has often been claimed. The famous British warning to Washington of 21 February 1947 was precipitated primarily by inter-departmental wrangling in London, and especially by Treasury pressure for economy. Bevin himself was anxious to be quit of Greece given the failings of successive governments in Athens. Admittedly he had reason to expect an American response of some kind, but even so the Foreign Office found it difficult to divest itself of its image of the Americans as a mercurial people whose 'archaic' constitution was yet another impediment to the pursuit of a consistent and long-term foreign policy. The manner in which Congressional approval was secured for the Truman Doctrine plus that document's strident pledges of American support for 'free peoples' threatened by subversion or outside pressures also caused some unease.[25]

Nevertheless more help from the United States was becoming imperative as Europe and Britain reeled under a savage winter early in 1947, and the problems of purchasing imports from dollar areas became ever more acute. Fortunately for the Western Europeans Soviet stalling tactics at a conference in Moscow in the spring of 1947 persuaded George Marshall, the American secretary of state, that the patient (Europe) was sinking while the doctors deliberated. There were growing fears in the State Department that Europe's dollar shortage could lead to autarkic policies, a neutral stance in the emerging Cold War, or – even worse – to such low living standards and demoralisation that communist influence would increase in much of Western Europe, with or without direct Soviet intervention. More positively there were also those in the American government who believed that without the revitalisation of the economy of western Germany there could be no enduring or adequate recovery elsewhere in Europe. Yet any significant German revival would be unthinkable for the French without strong inducements from the United States. At the same time it was appreciated by the State Department that Congress was unlikely to foot the bill unless clear evidence was forthcoming from the Europeans that American money would be well spent. It was here that Bevin's reaction was so important. He responded quickly and imaginatively to discreet signalling from Dean Acheson in Washington to the effect that positive action by the Europeans was needed to impress Congress. But if he acted first the French were not far behind. Furthermore the British would have preferred to separate themselves as far as possible from the rest of Europe, arguing that their world commitments entitled them to special treatment in Washington. The Treasury even examined the possibility of doing without aid rather than accept the American demands for a co-operative European effort. The unrealism of such a choice soon became apparent.[26]

This sign of British aloofness from Europe, however, raises the vexed question of the degree to which Britain was already parting company from other Western European states, and was thereby forfeiting her opportunity to play a leading part, perhaps the leading part in the creation of a more unified Europe. Here, conceivably, was the most important missed opportunity in post-war British foreign policy. Many have contended that priority was mistakenly given to national sovereignty (only for it to be constrained in different ways by the United States) and to her extra-European interests, choices which added to her foreign responsibilities in later years and robbed her both of the invigorating effects of deeper involvement in the European economies and of a more rapidly expanding market than that which the Commonwealth and Sterling Area could provide in the longer term. In contrast J. W. Young argues that until the middle of 1948 Britain was at least as European-minded as France, while other scholars have discovered ample justification for the decision of the British – given their perception of their nation's circumstances and prospects in the late 1940s – to place strict limits on their European commitments. At that time they had reason to suppose that their existing priorities were the right ones.[27]

By 1948 the Foreign Office was certainly becoming more conscious of the decline of Britain's power in the world and was less confident that this decline could be reversed. The creation of the Western European Union early in 1948 stirred some fresh hopes that, after a perod of indispensable American assistance, the Europeans – and especially the British – might be able to exercise greater influence over their own destiny. But this phase soon passed. In any case Britain was reluctant to accept any but the loosest ties with Europe. Bevin opposed any talk of European federalism. His earlier interest in a European customs union was now seen to be irreconcilable with Britain's special trading relations with the Commonwealth. The Treasury and Board of Trade were particularly hostile to European collaboration, and for the time being they were able to argue from current and projected figures that Britain would fare better by giving priority to extra-European trade. Only a quarter of Britain's trade was with Europe – less than in the 1930s. European integration, it was feared, might add to the drain on hard currencies from Britain.[28] It was believed that the primary products of much of the Commonwealth would command high prices for some time to come, and that Britain would find it easier than the Europeans to obtain crucial raw materials. Within the Commonwealth and Sterling Area lay the best prospect of solving Britain's dollar problems, and in general it was expected that Britain's recovery would outpace that of her neighbours. Many British industries in any case preferred the sheltered Commonwealth markets. Neither the Treasury nor the Foreign Office looked far into the future, and neither foresaw the great growth in trade between the industrial nations of Europe or the limitations of Britain's traditional markets.[29]

The American recession of 1949 was a serious blow to the recovery of Britain and the Sterling Area, but the resultant economic crisis which led to the devaluation of sterling merely confirmed the trend away from Europe.[30] Devaluation was negotiated with Washington without regard for European interests, but it was not appreciated that while Washington was now ready to make special allowance for Britain's extra-European activities, it was at the same time encouraging steps towards Western European integration – if necessary without Britain. The Schuman Plan for the creation of a European Coal and Steel Community thus emerged in 1950 with American blessing to the consternation of the British who had been left in ignorance on the sidelines. Nevertheless much as this rankled the British had already settled their own priorities. The Foreign Office by March 1949 had conclusively abandoned any hopes of the emergence of a 'third world power'. It feared excessive German influence in a united Western Europe, and insisted that, whenever a choice had to be made between Europe and the United States, Britain should always opt for the latter.[31] Bevin himself in

October 1949 emphatically placed Europe third after the United States and the Commonwealth in Britain's priorities.

Admittedly the British might have responded a little more positively to the Schuman Plan had it not been for its supra-national dimension. Bevin objected to the idea of a European parliament, arguing that one should not try to 'put the roof on before we have built the building'. He likened supra-nationalists to 'Trojan horses'. Such institutions as the Organisation for European Economic Co-operation and the Council of Europe were more acceptable. Nor were the French necessarily less nationalistic than the British. Their thinking had been transformed by the failure of self-contained nationalist policies and equally – in their view – of such limited Europeanist experiments as the British seemed prepared to tolerate. Of necessity they became more adventurous, and in particular came to believe that they had a better prospect of regulating the economic revival of Germany within a multinational instrument such as the Schuman Plan. Alan Milward, despite his criticisms of British insularity and traditionalism, fully accepts the importance of chance in the movement of the Western Europeans towards the economic miracle of the 1950s. They had more incentive than the British to experiment, even if they also displayed more imagination and enterprise. As a result by the 1950s they were travelling along 'a more hopeful path towards future prosperity than the United Kingdom'.[32] Meanwhile Europeanists became an increasingly rare breed in the Britain of the late 1940s – exceptions within the Foreign Office being most noticeable among those with direct experience of the workings of the Organisation for European Economic Co-operation. By 1950 Bevin was arguing that Britain's policy in Europe should be guided essentially by what she needed to do in order to satisfy the United States. The American connection had become the 'kernel' of British foreign policy.

Stalin has sometimes been described as the person most responsible for the formation of Nato, and the same might be said of his contribution to the creation of the post-war Anglo-American relationship. A common enemy supplied Anglo-American relations with a postive energy which economic ties alone

would not have generated. The latter, indeed, tended to accentu-
ate the negative feelings which arose from British dependence
upon the United States in the early post-war years. In contrast
Britain's worldwide network of strategic bases, her possession of
greater economic and military power than any other possible
American ally before the later 1950s, and the expectation well
into the 1950s that a war with the USSR would mean the loss
of all or most of continental Europe, gave the British a special
value in American eyes. Even so the Attlee government did not
rush headlong into a choice of sides. Only at the end of 1947
did Bevin become sufficiently disturbed by Soviet conduct and
obstructionism to decide that some sort of Atlantic compendium
had become essential. Some association was now needed to
inspire the necessary degree of political and psychological confidence throughout Western Europe if Marshall Aid and the other
policies designed to rebuild parliamentary democracy were to
succeed. Even then some of the earlier ambivalence in British
attitudes towards the United States persisted. There was an
understandable nationalist desire to have the Americans on tap
rather than on top. But events from the winter of 1947–8
were supplying compelling reasons for some direct American
commitment to the defence of Western Europe. Britain began to
move from a policy of rebuilding British influence with *ad hoc*
American assistance towards a longer term and more comprehensive reliance upon the United States. It was rapidly becoming
an article of faith in the Foreign Office that British interests
could often be best promoted by the cultivation of as much
influence as possible in Washington.

Some scholars, nevertheless, still cast a baleful eye over British
policy-making, and ask if British and Western European interests
could not have been adequately protected with less militant
policies, and by a more selective relationship with the United
States. They do not wholly agree with Henry Pelling's claim
that Bevin's 'greatest achievement was the North Atlantic Treaty'
or K. O. Morgan's suggestion that this was one of the most
sustained creative periods in British foreign policy since the days
of the Elder Pitt.[33] The critics reply that these years might be
interpreted in other ways. Geoffrey Warner, in noting Bevin's

satisfaction at the inauguration of Nato, argues that it was achieved at a heavy price, so heavy that 'the historian is legitimately entitled to wonder whether there might have been other, less damaging ways of achieving the same objective'.[34] Elisabeth Barker suggests that there existed in Whitehall tendencies almost as strong as those in Washington to exaggerate the unity of the communist world (although she does acknowledge Bevin's efforts in 1949 to reopen a dialogue with the USSR – much to the dismay of the British chiefs of staff).[35] Others complain that Bevin helped to institutionalise the Cold War, and stress the fact that Britain was more hostile than either France or Italy to the USSR.[36] This was hardly surprising given the greater French fear of Germany, while, as in Italy, account had to be taken of large native communist parties and their sympathisers. In contrast by 1949 British critics of anti-Soviet policies had become a small and unimportant minority. Although Bevin continued to probe Soviet intentions, he now basically believed that the current status quo was the best that could be secured in Europe. At the official level one also suspects that enthusiasm for Nato was not a little influenced by the belief that this organisation would enable Britain to exercise greater influence over American policy.[37]

Bevin's critics are also in danger of anticipating developments. It is important to remember that Nato, until the widespread alarm produced by the outbreak of war in Korea in 1950, was viewed as a political rather than a military instrument. Thus, until the summer of 1950, British defence expenditure – though uncomfortably high – was based on the calculated gamble that there would be no worsening of the Cold War over the next few years. Exaggerated Western estimates of Soviet conventional military strength in Eastern Europe were not accompanied by high expectations of war at this time. Communist propaganda, communist influence among trade unionists in some Western countries, and the fragility of Western European morale even in 1950 were seen as the greater dangers to the West. Bevin reacted to the communist takeover in Czechoslovakia in February 1948 with the comment that communists could never be trusted to abide by the rules of Westminster once they had wormed their way into office. The serious unrest in France in the autumn of 1947 was fresh in his mind, and civil war did not seem an impossibility in Italy in the spring of 1948. Even so British Intelligence was moderately optimistic.[38] The containment of the USSR and communism became heavily reliant on military power only from 1950.

In fairness to Bevin it must also be remembered that when he began his search for an Atlantic community in the winter of 1947–8 he could not be certain what form the end product would take. Nor at that time could he foresee the Czech coup, the Berlin blockade and the Korean War. The Berlin crisis was sufficiently alarming for him briefly to feel some passing sympathy for Neville Chamberlain at the time of Munich. Negotiations once seriously begun for the organisation of some sort of Atlantic association did not proceed in a straight line, the extent of the American commitment and the number of European states to be included being matters for debate until the beginning of 1949. Decisions were often taken in response to immediate pressures, notably the British government's agreement at the height of the Berlin crisis to permit the stationing of American B-29 strategic bombers in Britain. This had much more far-reaching implications than were apparent at the time. In 1948 the intention was to remind the Kremlin that these aircraft could be equipped with atomic bombs and were an earnest of American's intention to stand firm in Europe. Only later, it seems, with the unexpectedly early Soviet nuclear test (in 1949) and with the obvious determination of the American air force, once re-established in Britain, to maximise its presence, was it seen that Britain might have exposed herself to exceptional dangers as an American front-line base. With no formal agreement the British government could not be sure that it would always be consulted before American aircraft were used in an emergency. Yet during the Berlin crisis it seemed sensible to send a firm signal to Moscow, especially when memories of Munich were fresh in so many minds. In the summer of 1948 an American commitment to Europe was welcomed, despite some reservations concerning American patience and level-headedness.

Nato as it took shape in 1948–9 owed a great deal to British and French influence, far more in fact than might reasonably have been expected from a simple comparison of their strength in relation to that of the United States. London and Paris were able to play upon divisions within the American administration as well as the widespread belief that Western Europe was vital to American security. If there were worries about undue American influence in the future, these were more than offset by the attractions of a virtual promise of immediate aid in a crisis.[39] Indeed in the spring of 1949, with the ratification of Nato and the ending of the Berlin Blockade, the Foreign Office had reason to feel that an equilibrium might at last be emerging in Europe, a view shared by some American diplomats. Meanwhile the British commitment to the defence of Europe remained hesitant, not least because the continent still seemed indefensible in the unlikely event of a serious Soviet attack. As late as 1951 a French general was complaining of the weakness of British forces in Europe and the uncertainty surrounding reinforcements to be expected in the event of an emergency.[40]

The British chiefs of staff preferred to work closely with the Americans even if they were not always sure what the Americans would do in an emergency. Bevin himself concluded in October 1949 that the Western European states would not be strong enough for at least ten years to hold back a Soviet assault while they waited for the United States to mobilise. With others he hesitated to follow Montgomery's advice that a realistic strategy in Europe required the rearmament of West Germany. Bevin remarked in August 1950 that 'people here were definitely doubtful of Europe'. Thus despite the formation of Nato Britain did not move closer to her European neighbours. Her defence strategy remained Atlanticist and Middle Eastern in its priorities. At the same time the British were often unable to do more than listen sympathetically to new American proposals relating to the more effective defence of the West. Thus in the spring of 1950 Bevin could only assure the American secretary of state that he did not indefinitely rule out discussion of the rearmament of West Germany, a minor advance on the blank negative delivered by the French. These delaying tactics were possible as Washington itself was still groping for a policy.[41]

Perceived Cold War needs were similarly shaping British policy far beyond the Atlantic, Europe and the Middle East. Despite the moves of a new South African government towards apartheid, the Labour cabinet continued to cultivate close political and defence ties for the security of imperial interests in Africa and the alternative route to the Far East. Fears that communism might be undermining the European colonial empires in South-East Asia also found the British in 1948–9 looking impatiently for some American involvement in this region. Indeed the British anticipated the American fears of the 1950s that the peoples and states of this region might fall in 'domino' fashion to communist assault and subversion. They fully subscribed to the view that the leader of the Vietminh against the French colonial power in Indo-China, Ho Chi Minh, was a dedicated Moscow-dominated communist. Given their own problems in and fears for Malaya, one of the most prized components of the Sterling Area (its exports in 1950 represented about one-quarter of sterling earnings), the British were naturally anxious to preserve a buffer to the north. The strength of the French and their local allies in Indo-China was precarious, so that an American involvement of some kind seemed imperative.[42] The Foreign Office acknowledged that any partnership here with the United States might soon be an unequal and an expensive one. But risks had to be run to protect precious British assets.

Nevertheless the British were not afraid to show their independence of Washington. The communist victory in 1949 in China excited considerable alarm, and Mao's regime was perceived to be truly Marxist–Leninist. Even so the Foreign Office favoured recognition of the *fait accompli*, despite American objections, and despite Colonial Office fears that recognition might encourage the Chinese insurgents in Malaya. British commercial interests in China, actual and potential, were given priority, together with the desire to please Asian nationalists, and especially the newly independent state of India. But in the spring of 1950 it was acknowledged that neither the British approach nor the American was making any impression on the Chinese communists.

The Korean War, which broke out in June 1950, intensified both the British dependence upon the United States and the

British desire to guide American policy into acceptable directions. At one level the American action in Korea suggested that the United States could be relied upon to give prompt and effective support to its friends. At another it was feared that the United States might be tempted to reduce its military presence in Europe in order to fight a war for a country which strategically was of no interest to Britain. To this were soon added fears of American recklessness and ambition. A conflict fought initially to persuade Moscow that military aggression anywhere would not be tolerated by the West seemed in danger of escalating into a major war in its own right. In fairness to the United States it must, however, be acknowledged that when the North Korean occupation of much of the South collapsed in September 1950, Bevin was among those who at first failed to anticipate that the Chinese would resist any attempt to turn the whole of Korea into a pro-Western state. He expected the main danger to lie in a Soviet bid to regain the political initiative. He was also anxious to act in a way that would satisfy Washington and reinforce the American commitment to Europe and to Britain.[43] Any British suggestions for caution came too late to influence the outcome.

Even the first stage of the Korean War had not been without its embarrassments. The British shared some of the American fears that Korea might merely be the first of a series of probing, aggressive moves by the communist bloc. But an admission that some rearmament was necessary did not mean that London welcomed all the ambitious plans emanating from Washington. The rearmament of West Germany was now an explicit American priority, and one which was supported by the British chiefs of staff. But this was still a highly controversial issue in Britain, not least in the Labour Party. The British finally gave rather equivocal support to the United States, but were perhaps not totally displeased by French delaying and spoiling tactics. International tension, however, was sharply increased by the dramatic and highly successful Chinese intervention in the Korean War in November 1950. Chinese success, it seemed, might provoke a dramatic American escalation of the war, perhaps to the nuclear level, and also result in the diversion of American military strength to the Far East at the expense of

Europe. Inevitably anxious questions were asked about likely Russian responses either in support of China or in the form of new adventures elsewhere in the Middle and Near East or even in Europe. Western rearmament now seemed all the more imperative, despite worries that the start of a massive military build-up in Europe might precipitate the very collision with the USSR which it was intended to deter. After the Soviet nuclear test in 1949 American nuclear weapons no longer seemed so assured a deterrent, and in any case they were not expected to save Europe from Soviet occupation and a long war of liberation comparable to that of 1939–45. Yet even at this stage, on 2 December, Bevin also appeared fearful of a very different sort of Soviet offensive, one designed to divide the West and slow Western rearmament. He feared any developments which could lead to the dissolution of Nato and to an American withdrawal from Europe.[44] It was thus for a variety of reasons that the cabinet on 18 December agreed to a large increase in defence spending. Greater British military power was needed to encourage allies in Europe. It was also deemed necessary to impress and satisfy the United States. Finally it was hoped that from a position of strength a truly lasting and stable East–West settlement might ultimately be negotiated.[45]

A close watch was still kept on American policy. Attlee hastened to Washington early in December 1950 following remarks by Truman which suggested that Washington had not ruled out the use of nuclear weapons in all circumstances in the current conflict in the Far East. The reassurances which he received did not put an end to an uneasiness which was by no means confined to those who were naturally inclined to distrust the United States. One of Bevin's last acts as foreign secretary was to combat a suggestion in the cabinet that the time might come when Britain should distance herself from the United States – at least in the Far East. Bevin denied that it was in the American character to provoke war. Isolationism was still the greater danger to British interests: persistent Allied carping and opposition might encourage its revival. But the debate on Anglo-American relations continued in the cabinet after his resignation and death, while controversy over the cost of rearmament and economies in the National Health Service led to the resignation of Aneurin Bevan, the idol of the left. Directly and indirectly foreign affairs contributed to the decision to hold an election in October 1951 and to Labour's narrow defeat.

Those who defended the American connection were reassured by the increases in American forces in Europe in 1951. American support for the French in Indo-China was also welcome, while the sacking of General MacArthur in April 1951 for disobedience in the conduct of the Korean War somewhat diminished fears of an all-out conflict between the United States and China. Nevertheless British and Allied influence over American conduct in the Far East was diminishing. Despite the cease-fire talks in Korea from June 1951, the Truman administration continued upon occasion to weigh the pros and cons of intensifying the war against China. The use of nuclear weapons was not excluded. Rosemary Foot argues that 'Allied opinion lost influence to the point that the United States contemplated a limited reduction of its European commitments in order to effect a military end to the conflict in Korea.'[46] Britain's pride took a further fall in 1951 when Australia and New Zealand independently entered into a defence pact with the United States (ANZUS).

Even the depth of the American commitment to the defence of Europe was not without its complications, notably the growing American reliance on air bases in the United Kingdom. British hopes of closer collaboration with the United States in nuclear matters – perhaps even to the extent of being provided with nuclear bombs by the Americans – evaporated in 1950, whereas the Korean crisis brought a great expansion in the American military presence in Britain. Attlee's visit to Washington in December 1950 was designed in part to clarify the conditions surrounding the use of British bases, but in so far as an understanding was reached it could at best be described as 'deliberately fuzzy'.[47] September 1951 found Herbert Morrison (Bevin's successor) complaining in Washington that it was intolerable that Britain should be threatened with annihilation without representation. Yet the most that the Americans would concede was a promise that if possible a joint decision would be taken in an emergency. Simon Duke concludes that the Attlee government 'left as its legacy perhaps the most important defence commitment made by one first-class power to another'.[48] At bottom the British were obliged to choose between an American nuclear presence – over which they could not be certain to exercise ultimate control – or its removal, with the accompanying risk of a reduced or even the liquidation of the American presence in Europe. To have chosen the latter course would also have implied less – if any – British influence in Washington. A massive question mark would have been placed against the emerging balance in Europe, both between East and West and within Western Europe itself where the potential strength of West Germany was already causing concern. Thus, given their respective needs, the British and Americans had reached a point, both on the question of bases in Britain and on consultation prior to American use of nuclear weapons, where a satisfactory formal agreement was unattainable. The British, as the weaker party, had to draw such comfort as they could from American assurances, not commitments. The position, it would seem, has not substantially altered since 1951.

Under Attlee and Bevin between 1945 and 1951 decisions of far-reaching importance had been taken in British foreign policy. Despite pressing demands for the development of the welfare state and for full employment, despite major domestic and international economic problems, and despite controversy within the Labour Party, the government had chosen to minimise the reductions in Britain's world role. It had agreed to accord defence a higher priority than had been the case with British governments after the First World War. In particular it had decided that in some form or other Britain should become one of the world's nuclear powers. In the view of Lord Bullock this government had not only advanced British interests and influence since 1945, but had done so without imposing excessive strains upon the nation's resources. It had also left its successors a range of choices. Elisabeth Barker agrees that its achievements were 'far bigger than the country's actual strength warranted'.[49]

On the other hand it has been suggested that the Cold War was 'almost a blessing' for those eager to preserve Britain's role as a world power. Success in 1948–9 encouraged the belief that a similar measure of influence could be exercised in the future. Success blinded policy-makers to changing circumstances and alternative ways forward – such as closer ties with Western European states. Even in the formation of Nato Britain's part was perhaps not indispensable. The British exaggerated American inexperience and naïveté, and likewise the faint-heartedness of the Europeans.[50] Recently there have come pleas for more sympathetic assessments of the alternative policies suggested by many on the left of the Labour Party, and especially their complaints of British subservience to the United States in 1951 and the relative neglect of social and economic reform. Elisabeth Barker herself suggests that Bevin might have missed an opportunity to negotiate a *modus vivendi* with the USSR before 1950.[51] Much of this is fair comment, but just as the British leaders exaggerated the nation's influence in one way, so some of their critics tend to exaggerate its potential in another. British post-war influence peaked in 1947–9, and even then it owed much to the existence of groups in Washington who were disposed to move in the same direction. Britain lacked the time before the Korean War – and probably the means – to ease her relations with the USSR.[52] As for the war itself, it took time to assess its implications and to decide whether or not it represented a truly sinister change in the character of the Cold War.

# 4

# REAPPRAISALS AND
# READJUSTMENTS

CONSERVATIVE delight on their return to office in October 1951 was tempered by the smallness of their parliamentary majority and by the magnitude of the economic problems (notably the balance of payments deficit) confronting the country. At the same time they were expected to preserve the welfare state and put an early end to austerity and rationing, while they themselves wished to uphold and even enhance Britain's position in the world. Churchill himself naturally had no intention of presiding over the liquidation of Britain's role as a world power, and if the most extreme upholders of this pretension were to be found in the Conservative Party, in some form or other it was a role which large sections of the British public continued to cherish. Thus suggestions from the Treasury and to some extent from the Foreign Office that Britain was carrying too many foreign responsibilities in relation to her resources failed to elicit more than ambiguous and hesitant responses – at best – from leading ministers. This was particularly true of the new foreign secretary. Although Eden sometimes acknowledged the need for more selectivity (and he did indeed push through an agreement with Egypt on the future of the Suez base in 1954), he often found pressing reasons why current policies should be pursued a little longer.

The new government enjoyed some good fortune. It was able to take speedy advantage of the lessening tension between East and West, especially as the war in Korea settled down to a stalemate. It was increasingly assumed by Western leaders that, as the fear of war with the USSR receded, so it was appropriate to think in terms of an enduring but probably controllable Cold War rather than of a rapid build-up in anticipation of a make-or-break crisis within the next two or three years. Defence cuts were thus possible, and contemporaries found themselves confronted by the fascinating spectacle of Churchill retrenching a Labour rearmament programme. A partial easing of Cold War tensions also meant that Churchill was soon able to begin his search for better relations with the USSR. In contrast he found it much more difficult to come to terms with the challenges offered by the swelling nationalist forces in the Middle East.

Nevertheless economic difficulties loomed so large that at times even a Churchill cabinet found itself discussing the case for and against a radical reappraisal of Britain's overseas commitments. The Treasury issued a bleak warning on 23 May 1952 that it could see only 'a continuing mountain of difficulties' beyond 1953, and claimed that Britain would either have to cut her foreign commitments or increase the value of exports by one-fifth. In the absence of either it implied that it would be necessary to reduce government expenditure so drastically at home that it would 'reshape the whole of our national life'.[1] The electoral implications were obvious. Defence was absorbing about 10 per cent of both the labour force and the gross national product, while new equipment for the armed forces was being produced at the expense of British engineering exports. The foreign secretary himself admitted on 18 June 1952 that current policies were in excess of the nation's resources, but counter-attacked with the argument that even a well-considered strategy of withdrawal abroad could result in damage to the British economy as well as in a decline in international status. He conceded that perhaps in the longer run, if the problems proved intractable, Britain might have to make a choice between the oil of the Middle East and the rubber of South-East Asia. In the meantime he hoped, with something short of complete confidence, to enlist more American aid in the regions in question.[2] Not surprisingly the chancellor – and other ministers – was not satisfied and returned to the question regularly over the next few years. Thus soon after the 1955 election the deteriorating economic situation provoked further warnings from the Treasury of renewed threats to the strength of the pound and of 'serious industrial and social strains at home' if welfare and civilian consumption were sacrificed in the interest of overseas commitments.[3]

The economies effected in the 1950s led, however, to adjustments rather than to radical changes in Britain's foreign commitments. Only over the course of two decades did they make a significant impact. Meanwhile at this time the main influence upon grand strategy was the rapid development of nuclear weapons and the impending introduction of long-range missiles. Hitherto for the British a nuclear capability of their own had been something which lay in the future: the West's nuclear deterrent was the monopoly of the United States. But the British could now confidently expect to be in possession of their own strategic nuclear force before the end of the decade, together with British-made battlefield or tactical weapons. In the same period, however, the superpowers would be acquiring thermonuclear bombs and warheads, and megatonnage weaponry of this kind would make nonsense of current preparations for a lengthy war. Fission bombs in the kiloton range, despite their awesome power as demonstrated at Hiroshima, had failed to persuade most defence experts that they alone could determine the outcome of a global war – hence the massive stockpiling of strategic raw materials by the West in response to Korea. No defence, however, seemed conceivable against the H-bomb. It was anticipated that Britain would be crippled in a matter of days. As early as the summer of 1952 the British chiefs of staff produced a remarkable paper on the implications for Britain's armed forces and defence policy, although nearly five years were to elapse before their ideas began to be systematically introduced.

In 1952 the defence chiefs were also suggesting that war with the USSR was improbable – except by accident. They envisaged a long-drawn-out Cold War, so that defence expenditure had to be guided by what the national economy could readily sustain. A strategy built around nuclear deterrence was essential for military reasons, but it carried with it the added promise of significant financial savings. Simultaneously there existed a strong and natural desire to escape from total dependence upon the American nuclear arsenal. A defence review transmitted to the cabinet on 2 November 1954 concluded that the prime task of the envisaged nuclear bomber force (of some 240 aircraft) would be the destruction of those Soviet air bases which posed a direct threat to Britain. Soviet conventional forces in the heart of Europe might also be a secondary military objective. There was in addition an important political dimension. A nuclear capability was regarded as one of the most effective means whereby the British could command attention in Washington. Equally it was seen as a prerequisite if Britain were to continue to obtain a seat at the top table with the superpowers.[4] The chiefs of staff themselves reiterated the popular justification for a British role at the highest level when they insisted that American 'experience, judgement and internal political system' were all ill-adapted to the great international responsibilities they were asked to bear.[5] Thus statements from the Treasury to the effect that British foreign and defence policies were imposing excessive burdens upon the economy were bluntly countered by the political argument that it was imperative that Britain should be in possession of the means to speak with authority in the world – even at great cost to the nation.

A number of apparent successes in British foreign policy in 1954, the high point of Eden's career as an international statesman, came to the assistance of those who argued that it was in the national interest that Britain should continue to bear the responsibilities of a great power and cultivate influence in Washington. Two long-running Middle Eastern disputes – with Egypt and Iran – were finally resolved on reasonably satisfactory terms with some assistance (not always consistent) from the United States. Much more striking was Eden's part in the negotiation of a cease-fire between the French and the Vietminh (or communist-led insurgents) in Indo-China, and in the resolution of the crisis in Europe occasioned by the French refusal to join the European Defence Community. In the last two instances it was possible to argue that the British had followed a more statesmanlike course than the Americans. The West had been spared a new Korean War in South-East Asia, while the rearmament of West Germany could now proceed with the consequential strengthening of Nato's conventional forces. British foreign policy might be costly, but it was earning dividends and sparing Britain possibly ruinous expenditure at some time in the future. In 1954 it also seemed possible to make a more optimistic projection of the nation's economic prospects. A dramatic improvement in the terms of trade was for the time being relieving the strain on the balance of payments. Perhaps a pass was opening up through the 'continuing mountain' of economic difficulties.

While the British were in danger of exaggerating the solidity of their own achievements, their special position in Washington in the 1950s was nevertheless protected by the fact that no other member of the Western alliance had so many means and opportunities at its disposal to compel or attract the attention of the American government. In Europe, admittedly, Washington was particularly interested in West Germany, but the Nazi shadow still lay across that country, inhibiting its political influence, while its resurgent economic power was not as yet reflected in its military contribution to the defence of the West. The French, plagued by recurrent government crises, weakened by the war in Indo-China and later in Algeria, were failing to exert as much influence in Nato as might have been expected. Japan's economic miracle had scarcely begun, and she remained a negligible force in high politics.

Britain's special place beside the United States was thus prolonged even when other economies were beginning to advance more rapidly than her own. Furthermore, although many in the American government had little patience with Britain's pretensions, and were often critical of British policies, some of the old aura surrounding Britain's statecraft was still present. Thus Churchill's first visit to the United States (7–8 January 1952) after his return to Downing Street aroused not a little trepidation in the State Department. Much serious thought was given to ways to thwart his more ambitious demands.[6] Indeed memories were still fresh of the quick thinking required of Acheson and others when Churchill's less esteemed predecessor,

Clement Attlee, had wrung a damaging concession from President Truman during a visit at the end of 1950. Henry Kissinger, although his experience of diplomacy at first hand came much later, enthused over the diplomatic expertise of the British in this period. They insinuated themselves so effectively into the American decision-making process that they 'became psychologically impossible to ignore'. He also claimed that, for twenty years after the war, British wisdom and trustworthiness frequently persuaded American leaders – in their own self-interest – to take British advice on major questions. As secretary of state in the 1970s he regretted the weakening of the special relationship, not least because he feared the emergence of an increasingly united European Community.[7]

Yet diplomacy, however skilful, required physical backing, and it was a matter of some consequence, therefore, that Britain became the world's third nuclear power in the later 1950s. It is true that growing British reliance upon nuclear weapons soon led to reductions in the nation's conventional capabilities, especially in Europe. Such cuts were not well received by Britain's Nato allies. But from 1953 the Americans were also vulnerable to the same charge that they were looking to nuclear arms to reduce defence costs. Within Nato there developed a growing debate over the appropriate defence strategy for the West, and especially the degree to which nuclear weapons could or should be substituted for conventional arms. In practice, however, willingly or unwillingly, the members of Nato found themselves from the mid-1950s obliged to rely more and more on the nuclear deterrent, and compelled to look to tactical nuclear weapons to make good the deficiencies in the conventional forces deployed in the defence of the central front in Europe which they themselves were unwilling to rectify.

Meanwhile the USSR was rapidly expanding its nuclear weaponry directed at Europe, and it was also beginning to acquire an inter-continental capability. It was therefore tempting for the Americans to see in tactical nuclear weapons not only a partial substitute for conventional arms, but also, if a distinction could be drawn between tactical and strategic weapons, a means of reducing the danger that a war in Europe might escalate to embrace the territory of the United States. Such a prospect not unnaturally caused dismay in the British cabinet. As early as 5 April 1955 the foreign and defence secretaries jointly warned ministers of the dangers arising out of the American eagerness to draw such distinctions. They argued:

> The time is coming when Western forces will only be able to fight a global war with nuclear weapons. The decision to use these weapons will remain under political control. It is not possible to draw any definite dividing line between small and large nuclear weapons. Even if it were possible to do so, it would be gravely against our interests.[8]

Ministers feared that the USSR might be more tempted to risk war in Europe if it had reason to think that nuclear exchanges could be confined to the heart of Europe.

In the narrower context of Anglo-American relations Churchill entertained quite unrealistic hopes about the possibility of co-operation over nuclear strategy. Too much had happened since the war years. Nevertheless the United States now had to take Britain seriously as an emergent nuclear power, not least in order to try to exercise more control over the latter as she steadily acquired an effective strike force. While Churchill was unable to secure a totally binding agreement to joint decision in all circumstances before nuclear bombers were unleashed from American bases in Britain, the British were at last in receipt of some information relating to the American strategic air plan against the USSR. The American Atomic Energy Act of 1954 included further concessions, and thereafter the exchange of nuclear information quickened. In 1956 the Royal Navy received details of the new American submarine reactor, and in 1957 the two air forces began to discuss the allocation of targets for co-ordinated nuclear attacks on the USSR. When it seemed that the development of the American inter-continental B-52 bomber might lessen the dependence of the Strategic Air Command on bases in Britain, the start of the missile era in 1957 temporarily tipped the balance back again. The first generation of American missiles lacked the range to reach the USSR from the United States, and Britain agreed to act as one of the European host countries for such rockets under joint Anglo-American control. The United States had other base requirements in Britain, and most significantly of all from 1960 American nuclear submarines equipped with Polaris missiles began to operate from the Holy Loch in Scotland.

But however close the Anglo-American nuclear relationship, the British government became convinced of the need for an independent deterrent; Duncan Sandys as minister of defence in 1957, for instance, arguing that this must be developed in preparation for the time when the United States could rely on inter-continental missiles (ICBMs) alone. The Americans might then feel less inclined to honour their military guarantees to Europe. Britain was thus in the process of developing a more ambitious nuclear strategy, a significant advance upon that of the early 1950s when only a modest contribution to the Western deterrent had been envisaged.[9] Yet, paradoxically, dependence upon the United States was continuing to increase, notably in 1960 with the cancellation of Britain's intermediate range Blue Streak missile which faced obsolescence before its completion in the 1960s. A substitute threat to the USSR was sought in the extension of the life of the V-bomber force by the purchase of the stand-off Skybolt missile then under development in the United States. With Skybolt the V-bombers might hope to strike at Soviet cities without exposing themselves to the rapidly improving Soviet air defences.

Only two years later, however, the Kennedy administration decided that this missile was surplus to requirements. Its cancellation threatened to destroy British pretensions to remain an 'independent' nuclear power. The prestige and even the survival of the Macmillan administration in Britain were said to be at stake. Macmillan at a meeting with Kennedy in Nassau at the end of 1962 drew upon every weapon of influence and persuasion in his armoury, and to the dismay of many of Kennedy's advisers – who profoundly hoped that Britain's days as an 'independent' nuclear power were numbered – he finally persuaded the president to provide Britain with Polaris missiles so that Britain could develop her own underwater deterrent. He thus perpetuated the British 'independent' capability for at least one more generation. In many ways it was a remarkable diplomatic triumph for Macmillan.

In the first stage of its life Polaris was relatively cheap and, at a time when aircraft were becoming more vulnerable on land and in the air, the chances of these missiles reaching their target were high compared with anything which the V-bombers might have delivered. The true meaning of 'independence' was, however, much debated. Britain drew upon American technology, expertise and even upon American Intelligence. In the last resort, however, the submarines were under British control. In the longer term possession of Polaris and the special nuclear relationship with the United States facilitated the acquisition of the succeeding system, Trident, planned to become operational in the early 1990s. On the other hand ties with the United States were an obstacle to nuclear co-operation with France.

Britain's deterrent and her close relationship with the United States provoked strong protests at home, and for a time in the early 1960s the Campaign for Nuclear Disarmament reached formidable proportions. At one point it seemed that the unilateralists might be about to capture the Labour Party itself. But the Labour leader, Hugh Gaitskell, fought back vigorously, while his successor, Harold Wilson, presided over a ministry from 1964 which chose to proceed with the Polaris programme. Critics of this policy were not confined to the extreme left in British politics. Both Conservative and Labour cabinets, however, continued to rely on the national deterrent because, whatever the question marks which might be placed against this weapon and whatever the difficulties ministers might have in explaining its value and utility in hypothetical situations, in the last resort they could not bear to divest themselves of so awesome an instrument. As Joseph Frankel argues, British nuclear capabilities could not be ignored by either superpower, and they introduced 'an element of risk which could act as at least a partial restraint on some potential Soviet actions'.[10] Or such was the hope. Money saved by the abandonment of the deterrent and spent on conventional forces would not, successive governments believed, provide them with the same measure of security, or so much influence in Nato and in Washington. There was doubtless, too, the unspoken calculation that Britain might not be wholly powerless if by some mischance Nato were ever to collapse.[11]

In practice British conduct confirmed – if any confirmation were necessary – President de Gaulle in his determination both to try to exclude Britain from Europe and to go his own way in the creation of a French nuclear capability. On a wider front, British emphasis upon nuclear weapons at the expense of conventional forces troubled most of her Nato partners. A. J. R. Groom claims that Britain sabotaged 'all semblance of an attempt to provide a considerable conventional option in Central Europe'.[12] But responsibility for this failure surely cannot be laid at the door of the British alone. As it was Britain was troubled by the Deutschemark costs of those forces which were deployed in West Germany. Groom does, however, argue persuasively that the government in its overall defence policy was guilty of manipulating strategic doctrine and 'stretching' the armed forces to conceal fundamental deficiencies. The emperor was only partially clad whatever he might pretend to the contrary.

Meanwhile fear of nuclear war in the 1950s reinforced the natural instinct of British governments to seek accommodation with the USSR and communist China wherever possible. As Churchill wrote in 1954, 'The British people would not easily be influenced by what happened in the distant jungles of South-East Asia [a reference to the serious crisis in Indo-China in 1954]; but they did know that there was a *powerful American base in East Anglia* and that war with China, who would invoke the Sino-Russian Pact, might mean an assault by hydrogen bombs on these islands.'[13] The chiefs of staff warned the cabinet in October 1953 that in a third world war 'the main weight of the Soviet strategic attack will initially be directed against these islands' (as yet Britain did not possess her own deterrent) and would be the equivalent of a knock-out blow. They were unsure whether the growing nuclear arsenals would make for peace or war, although they believed that Stalin's successors were in no position to pursue an adventurous foreign policy. A year later Lord Slessor, formerly chief of the air staff, wrote more optimistically in his *Strategy for the West* of the prospects of agreement with the USSR, given the fear of nuclear war. He believed a new Locarno-type settlement might be possible for all Europe.[14] Shortly before his retirement as prime minister in 1955 Churchill also spoke hopefully of the future. If nuclear deterrents could be rendered immune from surprise attack, no power could hope to gain an advantage by striking first. It followed that a greater measure of stability should then be possible in East–West relations. In time safety might prove 'the sturdy child of terror, and survival the twin brother of annihilation'.

Churchill had tried to open up a dialogue with the East in 1953 following the death of Stalin. But American policy was, if anything, becoming more dogmatic in the hands of John Foster Dulles, secretary of state to the new Republican administration under President Eisenhower. The Korean War and McCarthyism discouraged flexibility. Meanwhile even within his own cabinet, according to one well-placed observer, the prime minister had to brave the 'displeasure' of colleagues, and threats of resignation. Churchill in retaliation mocked the advice of the Foreign Office from Anthony Eden downwards, only to be thwarted by his own ill-health as well as by American objections.[15] The Foreign Office wished to negotiate with the USSR from a position of greater strength, pressing for a delay at least until West Germany had been firmly welded into Nato. Once this was achieved in 1955, Eden, now translated to No. 10 Downing Street, was quick to follow Churchill's course – though in the face of similar objections from Washington. As one American complained, Eden shared the 'underlying characteristic' of all British ministers – 'that almost inbred, instinctive effort, in any collision, great or small, to find a compromise solution'.[16] This characterisation of the British was doubtless sharpened by Eden's part in the negotiation of an end to the hostilities in Indo-China in 1954. Some Americans believed that they had been deprived of a splendid opportunity to deliver a smashing blow against communism in South-East Asia. In contrast fears of all-out American intervention in this theatre had prompted Lord Salisbury, a leading figure on the right-wing of the Conservative Party, to speculate that the United States might (in 1954) pose a greater threat than the USSR to world peace.[17]

Despite such fears the British cabinet itself hoped that part of Indo-China could be saved from communism. Contingency plans existed for a British advance into southern Thailand if communist forces began to threaten Malaya from the north. At the same time ministers sensed the possibility of a compromise, given French war-weariness in the long struggle against the anti-French Vietminh forces under Ho Chi Minh. They also detected signs that the USSR might be willing to negotiate. Although some territory would be lost to communism (a concession with which the Eisenhower administration refused to associate itself), a compromise might yet provide sufficient safeguards for Western interests. Such a course seemed preferable to all the risks which the more aggressive factions in Washington seemed willing to run through some sort of military intervention. Indeed the British government increasingly feared that it was being asked to help persuade a divided American Congress to approve a military operation whose efficacy it doubted, and which might carry with it the danger of a third world war. Far better that Eden should seek a compromise – even if no more than an interim settlement resulted – at a projected conference in Geneva. Only in the light of its outcome might some sort of defensive alliance to protect Western interests in this region seem appropriate. But to Foster Dulles and others this was pure defeatism.

Divisions in Washington make it difficult to evaluate the importance of the British role. Eisenhower was torn between the desire to act decisively and the fear of plunging into another Asian quagmire without reliable and adequate allies. The army chief of staff and many in Congress were even more cautious or sceptical. Thus the British and the French (who were anxious for peace without a total loss of face) strengthened or confirmed the fears of the doubtful factions in Washington. With the United States in effect withdrawing to the sidelines at Geneva, the way was clear for Eden, the French, Russians and Chinese to negotiate. Eden himself, though often critical of the Americans, thought that their possession of the H-bomb contributed to the remarkable restraint shown by the USSR. Vietminh dependence on the major communist powers forced it to compromise. Consequently conditions prevailed in which Eden and his advisers could use their diplomatic and drafting skills to full advantage. Admittedly the resultant settlement was precarious and its terms were open to more than one interpretation. Eden himself may have had some doubts about its durability. His efforts to build a broader based agreement – a sort of Far Eastern Locarno – were vetoed by the Americans intent upon having no direct dealings with the Chinese.

One of Eden's biographers, David Carlton, uncharitably describes his role as 'unheroic', while strong Western opponents of communism at the time saw him as guilty of another Munich. Alternatively it can be argued that a breathing-space was negotiated, a breathing-space in which a progressive regime might conceivably have emerged in the non-communist south of Vietnam and, in co-operation with Cambodia and perhaps Laos, have worked towards the creation of a neutralist belt of states. Doubtless the communists of North and South Vietnam would still have set out to destabilise the South, but the outcome could hardly have been worse than that which resulted. From the British point of view, however, the less speculative effects were the injury this episode inflicted on Eden's relationship with Dulles. The British leaders were also fortified in their faith in their own superior wisdom. This was not the best preparation for the bigger challenge awaiting them in 1956.[18]

Meanwhile the British joined the American sponsored South-East Asian Treaty Organisation in September 1954, but they did so with mixed feelings, and Seato never realised the expectations of its founders. Sino-American relations continued to disturb the British, and London feared that Washington's venomous hostility towards the Chinese might result in some military stroke out of all proportion to the point at issue. Churchill explained his concern to the cabinet in a long memorandum of 2 August 1954 shortly after the conclusion of the Indo-Chinese settlement. He feared that some Americans might be tempted to exploit their current strategic nuclear advantage – one which they might enjoy for only another two or three years. If they sought a showdown with communist China, this in its turn might lead to general war. An American global victory could very well leave the British and the Western Europeans in the position of victims, 'whatever we thought, said or did'. On the brighter side he hoped that the USSR's temporary nuclear inferiority might open the way to creative talks. General fear of a nuclear disaster might even provide a foundation for twenty years of 'peaceful co-existence' from which one might proceed to the creation of a better and stabler world order. In striking contrast to this bold forward-looking exercise in high politics Churchill also indulged in some short-term domestic political calculation. He was troubled by a visit of Attlee and Bevan to Moscow, an episode which he feared might improve Labour's image in the eyes of the electorate. It was imperative that the Conservatives should demonstrate that they were equally committed to peace.[19]

At this time the relaxation of tension between East and West in Europe seemed partly dependent upon a similar relaxation in the Far East. The British, however, were unable to narrow the gulf which divided Peking and Washington.[20] Even in the context of Soviet-American relations from 1953 it often seemed as if the British were ploughing the sands, especially when the much trumpeted Paris Summit collapsed in failure in 1960. Sir William Hayter, the British ambassador in Moscow from 1953 to 1957, though impressed by the changes in style and atmosphere following Stalin's death, remained convinced that the 'new look' in Soviet foreign policy did not extend to matters of substance.

> The Soviet Government . . . were likely to adhere to their twin policies of consolidating their own extended empire and of undermining the rest of the world. They were talking of co-existence, but they visualized it as the co-existence of the snake and the rabbit.

Soviet methods to extend their influence were undoubtedly becoming more subtle, and he feared that Western leaders (by which he meant the British in the main) were all too eager to impress or reassure their own publics with initiatives to reduce tension. Only during the Hungarian crisis in 1956 did he think that British diplomacy might have been productive, an opportunity which was thrown away by the unfortunate Suez adventure.[21]

Eden and Macmillan, each in his turn as prime minister, saw the position very differently. Eden on 25 March 1955 argued that time was of the essence. The American public might become more isolationist once their country was threatened by intercontinental nuclear weapons. He did not trust the Germans in the long run, while the French had no consistent policy.

Communist adventurism was more likely in the Far East than in Europe, though the Soviets might try to divide the West with alluring new proposals on the future of Germany. He was also anxious to seize the initiative in order to convince public opinion in the West (and especially in Britain) of his government's determination to ease the Cold War. Thus he reported optimistically after meetings with the Soviet leaders later in the year, 'It is rather my impression that they regard us as the only possible bridge between themselves and the United States and that they are anxious that this bridge should be built.' A current Sino-American crisis was a good opportunity to demonstrate his sincerity of purpose to the Russians.[22] Similarly in 1955 Eden was anxious to find ways to reduce tension in the heart of Europe.

His proposals often displeased the Germans and the French. British eagerness to reduce their military commitments and to pursue Locarno-type mirages was equally worrying.[23] The Foreign Office was particularly interested in some form of military disengagement or thinning out in Central Europe to lessen the risk of an accidental collision. Nato's military experts, however, were convinced that any such agreements were likely to favour the USSR. It was widely feared in West Germany that concessions could lead to German neutralisation and the loss of American protection. Later, during Macmillan's visit to the USSR in 1959, Bonn complained that he was trying to bribe the British electorate at its expense. The Germans had a case. Macmillan was much influenced by domestic electoral considerations, a point he does not hide in his memoirs, especially when he believed that in so doing he had seized the initiative from the Labour Party in the run-up to the 1959 election. Of all the leading Western powers, Britain remained the most eager to conciliate the USSR during Khrushchev's attempts in 1958–61 to bully and manoeuvre the West into concessions on West Berlin and other German issues.

It is not possible to trace the impact of British conduct upon the Soviet leaders as it is upon Britain's allies in Nato. Although in the Berlin crises Khrushchev finally settled for the consolidation of East Germany by the erection of the Berlin Wall in August 1961, it is not unreasonable to assume that at times from

November 1958 he was testing the unity and resolve of the Western alliance. It is unlikely that Soviet motivation was ever a simple case of ambition or fear. There may thus have been times when British conduct encouraged the Kremlin to think of that nation as a weak link in the Western chain. Yet in general it is improbable that the British did much harm, and it was doubtless useful that one major Western nation should have tried to develop an East–West dialogue in a decade when others were so reluctant, and when it was important to establish what Stalin's successors really meant by 'peaceful coexistence'. Certainly over a period of years Britain's persistence would appear to have paid off in one area – namely in the slow and erratic progress towards the partial test ban of 1963. That treaty was, of course, profoundly influenced by the traumatic shock provided by the Cuban missile crisis of 1962, yet at the end of the day some American negotiators were prepared to acknowledge the persistent and painstaking contribution of the British to the ultimate success of those lengthy, complex and often stalemated talks. As one American participant, Glenn T. Seaborg, observed:

> Considering their relative unimportance as a military force, particularly in nuclear weapons, it is remarkable to consider how much influence the British had over United States arms and arms control policies during this period [1958–63].[24]

This was a very different view from that encountered by Arthur Schlesinger in the State Department in January 1962. At that time he frequently heard the complaint: 'We can't let Macmillan practise this emotional blackmail on us.' Macmillan, of course, could have made no progress had it not been for the interest of President Kennedy himself in an agreement. But, given the opposition of many of Kennedy's advisers to such talks, the British prime minister might well have encouraged the president to persevere.[25] Kennedy found Macmillan the most agreeable of the Western leaders of that era, although even he was occasionally heard to complain that Macmillan was too eager to play the peacemaker. Fortunately the British ambassador to Washington, Sir David Ormsby-Gore, was another favourite of a president who welcomed opportunities to seek advice and to discuss ideas with people whom he could trust outside his own government. Even during the Cuban missile crisis the opinion of the British was sometimes sought, although their actual influence on policy was small. Where the British probably achieved most, as Arthur Schlesinger notes specifically in the case of Ormsby-Gore, was in their reinforcement of Kennedy's own mounting scepticism 'about the clichés of the Cold War'.[26]

Such stress upon personalities, however, can only underline the precariousness of British influence in Washington. Thus Kennedy's successor was not inclined to look for outside advice, while Harold Wilson as leader of a Labour government in Britain from 1964 speedily lost the new president's confidence with his refusal of military support in the escalating Vietnam War, and as a result of the tactics he employed in the quest for a settlement to that conflict. But the Vietnam War was always likely to impose strains on Anglo-American relations. Macmillan himself had remained sensitive to British public opinion, and it had been his good fortune that no lasting contradictions developed between his interest in the cultivation of the United States and his domestic political needs – more often the opposite had been the case. By the end of the 1960s it was also evident that the United States could develop its own dialogue with the USSR (and even China) without British assistance. Furthermore, once Edward Heath became prime minister in the early 1970s and set out to carry Britain into the European Community, he was understandably anxious to demonstrate Britain's credentials as a good European state. Thus his administration was often distancing itself quite ostentatiously from the United States. Only with the return of Labour to power in 1974 was there some revival of the old intimacy.

Britain's transition from a power with extensive extra-European interests to one which gave primacy to her relationship with the EEC broadly coincided with the weakening of the special relationship with the United States. For many – scholars and others – Britain's belated entry into the EEC in 1973 is confirmation that the nation's governments had been pursuing the wrong priorities for many years – though they may disagree among themselves whether the fundamental mistakes were made in the late 1940s, the 1950s, or perhaps even in the 1960s. For others, however, it has been by no means self-evident that the right choice was made in the early 1970s. Given different interpretations of the national interest, and especially given stress upon national independence or upon the pursuit of socialist policies at home and abroad, Britain's entry into the EEC remains controversial despite the acknowledgement by the Labour leadership, after the Conservative electoral victory in 1987, of the permanence of British membership.

Britain's delayed movement towards Europe cannot be discussed in isolation from her continuing preoccupation with the empire, Commonwealth and other non-European commitments. It is true that from the end of the war one encounters occasional hints of interest in a rather closer relationship with Europe. Firmly as the Attlee government had clung to the African empire, it had at least debated Britain's role in the Middle East. Early in Churchill's last ministry warnings began to circulate that Commonwealth markets might be saturated by British exports in the not too distant future. Macmillan was among the few who began to ask if Britain could indefinitely reconcile her relations with the Commonwealth and with Western Europe. More than most he tried to weigh the implications for Britain of the closer co-operation which was beginning to develop among the states across the Channel.[27]

But in the early and mid-1950s the government was preoccupied with the defence of Britain's position outside Europe, and especially in the Middle East. By 1952 the British were under pressure from the American State Department to reappraise their policies in this region. Dean Acheson likened the situation to a couple locked in a warm embrace in a rowboat about to be swept over Niagara Falls. It was time to take to the oars and try to alter course.[28] This was a difficult period for the British. Crises developed simultaneously in 1951 with Iran over the nationalisation of the Anglo-Iranian oil company, and with Egypt over the future of the huge British base at Suez. Eden, for all his study of Oriental languages at Oxford, at first showed no more insight into Middle Eastern politics and emotions than his Labour predecessor in the Foreign Office. Indeed the latter, momentarily in his dealings with Iran, had seemed tempted to engage in a little good old-fashioned gunboat diplomacy. Eden himself failed to comprehend either the religio-nationalistic appeal of Dr Mussadiq in Iran or the secular charisma of the radical young officers who had recently seized power in Egypt. Meanwhile American patience was increasingly strained.

Nevertheless the two powers gradually reduced their differences, especially once the Americans were persuaded that a non-communist alternative to the Mussadiq regime was feasible in Iran (Iranian military forces with British and American covert assistance accomplished its overthrow in 1953), and when the British in their turn began to accept the need for concessions both to Iran and Egypt. Thus, whereas in February 1952 Eden was writing of the contribution – even in peacetime – of the Suez base to British 'influence and prestige throughout the Middle East',[29] a year later the Foreign Office was advising the cabinet that 'in the second half of the twentieth century we cannot hope to maintain our position in the Middle East by the methods of the last century'. The pressures for socio-political change in much of the Middle East were increasingly acknowledged. British policy in the future would require more local popular support. The chiefs of staff unequivocally agreed that it was too costly to hold the Suez base by force. Indeed as early as 1952 they had begun to argue that British interests in the Far East merited a higher priority. It was therefore essential to resolve differences with Middle Eastern states as far as possible.[30] Against the protests of a group of Tory backbenchers, and in the face of much grumbling from Churchill, an agreement was finally concluded with Egypt in October 1954 which, while providing for British evacuation of the base by 1956, also allowed for its reactivation in the event of outside aggression against Egypt, Turkey or the Arab League for a period of seven years. A settlement on the oil question had already been concluded with the new regime in Iran.

New difficulties, however, soon began to develop in the region. The British relationship with the Egypt of Colonel Nasser was never rooted in common interests. The British still aspired to exert major political and strategic influence in the Middle East, whereas Nasser was determined to bring about a progressive diminution in the influence of outside powers, and to emerge as the leader of progressive Arab nationalism. Both were thus too ambitious to co-exist. A collision was probably inevitable, but it was accelerated by the British decision to exploit the interest of the governments of Iraq and some other Middle Eastern states in a new defence alignment – the so-called Northern Tier whose consolidation was also being encouraged by the United States as a bulwark against the USSR. The British hoped that through membership of such an alliance they would be able to retain their cherished air bases in Iraq without giving hostages to radical Iraqi nationalists. The ill-fated Baghdad Pact was completed in April 1955. In Nasser's eyes this was a direct challenge, Iraq and Egypt being rivals for influence in the Middle East. Worse, the pact was a bid by Britain to preserve her influence in the region.

The Americans recognised that Western involvement in the pact could be counter-productive, but in Britain it excited almost no adverse comment. *The Economist* of 19 March 1955 was a rare exception. A Labour spokesman asserted that the Middle East was 'the Achilles' heel of the Commonwealth': a vacuum could not be tolerated.[31] A recent biographer of Eden suggests that the pact could have been 'a major turning-point' in the history of the Middle East, and applauds Eden's opportunism. This is a bold claim. The British move was understandable, but the vagaries and volatility of Middle Eastern politics were later to test the resources even of the superpowers. A closer relationship with one state or regime was often achieved only at the expense of strengthening enemies elsewhere. Turning-points tended to be transformed into corners within a maze with no centre. Eden himself acknowledged to the cabinet, before the pact was signed, that there would be difficulties, especially with Egypt. He also accepted at the time (a point forgotten by certain British ministers when they later criticised Washington's diffidence) that the United States was likely to stand aside – at least for the time being.[32] The pact might have been a justifiable gamble, but it was still a gamble, and the British were surely guilty of great recklessness when later in the year they tried to extend it to the then vulnerable state of Jordan.

Meanwhile rivalry with Egypt was leading to a debate within the British government on whether Nasser might yet be appeased, or whether, as Eden was inclined to think, he had to be weakened. In the end a further effort was made, in co-operation with the United States, to court Nasser with the offer of financial aid in the construction of the Aswan High Dam, a vast project designed to revolutionise the Egyptian economy. But in the first half of 1956 it speedily became apparent that Egypt could not be turned into a Western client state. When Nasser continued to flirt with communist countries (China proved the final straw), the United States (in July 1956) withdrew its offer of financial help. Nasser riposted with the nationalisation of the Suez Canal company, a blow against Britain, not the Americans. Not only did the British have a major stake in the company, but uninterrupted use of the canal was deemed vital given the amount of British trade – especially oil imports – which used that thread of water.

The initial reaction in Britain was one of almost universal outrage, and at first hopes ran high of productive co-operation with the United States to achieve a solution which would protect British interests. Yet only three months later opinion in Britain was confused and divided; relations with the United States were deteriorating; some members of the British government were intriguing with their French and Israeli counterparts to fabricate a crisis which would open the way to seizure of the canal by Anglo-French forces under the pretext of separating the warring armies of Israel and Egypt and protecting the Suez waterway. In practice, the seizure of part of the canal by Anglo-French units in the first week of November provoked almost universal condemnation at the United Nations. A humiliating withdrawal ensued, mainly, it would seem, as a result of American financial pressure on Britain. It was an extraordinary affair, and was the most evident post-war demonstration so far of the decline in British power. Not surprisingly the episode continues to excite controversy.

The strongest defence of British policy to be offered by a scholar to date is that by Robert Rhodes James. In particular he reveals from the cabinet papers that other ministers were not kept wholly in the dark by Eden and his closest associates, and that at least the broad lines of Eden's strategy received cabinet approval. Opposition was at best limited or ambiguous.[33] Most ministers, however, were not necessarily properly informed of the dangers foreseen by some experts, and notably of the warnings from the Treasury on the vulnerability of sterling. Ministers operated in an impressionistic world outside their own departments, and were easily swayed by preconceptions and emotions which modern scholars ignore at their peril. They were vulnerable to reminders of the lessons of the 1930s, and to warnings that Britain's status as a world power was at stake. It was easier for them to comprehend Nasser's challenge in this context rather than the detailed implications of the proposed remedies. Nasser's links with the USSR, for instance, readily aroused apprehension. The vulnerability of British oil supplies from the Middle East was a highly sensitive subject. The foreign secretary had earlier, in October 1955, drawn the cabinet's attention to a number of dangers in this area, while particular emphasis was laid upon an estimate that Britain's oil needs would treble over the next twenty years with the Middle East as the primary source.[34] Interestingly, at the same time he had stressed the need for close co-operation with the United States.

American foreign policy was the subject of much criticism in the late 1950s and thereafter, the critics coming to include such important American figures as Richard Nixon and Henry Kissinger. The irony is that the Eisenhower administration was itself deeply hostile to Nasser. It was, however, restrained by the fear that some injudicious action might throw the Middle East into the arms of the USSR. In response to the nationalisation of the canal Dulles therefore did his best to buy time. But the resultant mixture of ingenuity and ambiguity stood a chance of success only if the British were persuaded that Washington would, in the last resort, decisively oppose an appeal to arms. They did indeed receive warnings to that effect from various sources in Washington, including Eisenhower himself. But Eden and Macmillan were reluctant to accept these at face value, while all the time their impatience mounted in response to

Dulles's filibustering manoeuvres. Wishful thinking was very evident among the key policy-makers in London, and they were unmoved by warnings from the Treasury in September that the strength of the pound sterling was too fragile for Britain 'to go it alone'.[35] Macmillan, as chancellor, took note of the advice, but was more inclined to use the economic problems to argue that Britain could not afford to play for time in the way that Eisenhower recommended. Similarly he was determined to believe that in the end Eisenhower would not let Britain down. With Eden, he also hoped that a military operation would secure Nasser's overthrow as well as the canal itself.

Indeed, by 25 October some ministers – much to the dismay of the service chiefs – were making tentative plans for a lengthy occupation of parts of Egypt with up to four divisions (if necessary at the cost of withdrawing one division from Germany). Grand strategy was beginning to excite the imagination to a dangerous degree, with Macmillan, for instance, looking for a major expansion of Iraq to improve the pro-Western balance in the region.[36] Ministers were also pushed forward by the momentum imparted by earlier decisions. Once large forces had been concentrated in the Mediterranean, they could not be allowed to lie idle indefinitely. David Carlton suggests that Eden himself may have experienced occasional doubts only for them to be promptly nullified by the strength of feeling in the Conservative Party against any display of weakness. Eden's own position was not totally secure, with Macmillan as an obvious challenger for the premiership.

There is still some support for the contemporary claim that, if Britain had been able to use force immediately, success should have been attainable. Certainly the seizure of the canal itself was eminently feasible, but the Anglo-French forces would then have found themselves subjected to continuing irregular attacks, while the waterway itself remained vulnerable to sabotage. The allied presence would have been a continuing challenge to all radical nationalists in the Middle East. Gunboat diplomacy, even in the nineteenth century, was dependent for lasting success upon the political character of the people exposed to coercion, upon the readiness of the regime or its successor to bow to *force majeure*, and upon the absence of resistance from other quarters. Egypt had in practice been something of an embarrassment to the British from the moment of its occupation in 1882, itself the result of an unsuccessful naval bombardment. Lord Mountbatten, the First Sea Lord in 1956, was among those to identify such problems at the time without benefit of hindsight.[37]

The extent of other contemporary criticisms of government policy from professionals in the services, the Foreign Office and the Treasury is highly revealing – more so, indeed, than the assaults launched from the Opposition benches once the first surge of patriotic emotion following the nationalisation of the canal had subsided. Indeed some in the Labour Party were swayed more by practical objections than by the moral arguments publicly articulated at the time.[38] Yet for a Conservative cabinet even these practical objections, if fully understood, might still have suggested that further negotiations would have been a bolder and more difficult course than military action. Macmillan himself ordered the best defence, among many inadequate ones in his memoirs, when he emphasised the remoteness of the critics from the real world of decision-making. Had Britain no longer regarded herself as a great power, albeit of the second rank; and had the leading ministers not been dominated – as a result of their own experience and with the weight of the imperial past upon them – by outmoded beliefs as to how British interests could best be protected, the present might have been perceived as it was and not as Eden and Macmillan wished it to be. Suez may not be excusable but it is understandable.

Opinion differs as to whether Suez was a major or little more than a very melodramatic episode in modern British history. It is evident that its impact on the party political battle at home was short-lived: the Conservatives did not find it a liability in the 1959 election. It helped to accelerate the introduction of a defence policy which put more reliance on nuclear weapons, yet a re-examination of defence priorities had been under way for some time. Suez made Britain no more European-minded. Instead it persuaded Macmillan, the new prime minister from January 1957, to keep in closer step with the United States. Whatever the international humiliation suffered by the British at Suez the American president was soon eager to reciprocate. Questions had already been raised in Whitehall before Suez about the economic benefits of retaining parts of the East African empire, yet it was not until 1959 that any positive steps to accelerate decolonisation are discernible. Nationalists seeking to end colonial rule obviously drew encouragement from Suez, but Suez only gave a hearty push to causes which were already in motion. The British themselves also became rather more sensitive to local political feeling. The Foreign Office, for instance, began to take more interest in the reactions of the peoples around the Persian Gulf to the British presence. The Iranians, it was noted, found it 'an irritant'. As early as 1957 the foreign secretary was talking in the cabinet of the need for more flexible policies: more reliance should be placed on political rather than military influence.[39]

This did not mean that the British wholly eschewed military action. But they now tended to take more careful account of the local political situation. Of the various military actions in which they were involved during the next ten years, only that in Aden and the surrounding area turned out badly. The new flexibility was demonstrated by the Foreign Office's readiness in principle to enter into a dialogue with President Nasser in the early 1960s. Complaints from imperialist diehards that the British were losing the 'will to rule' – as if somehow by summoning up more 'will' the changes which were occurring in the Afro-Asian world could have been halted – miss the main point. The 'will to rule' from the eighteenth century had flourished in the context of great opportunities and rich incentives to govern. In the 1950s and 1960s the British increasingly found that whether or not force was effective in Afro-Asia, the rewards were often not commensurate with the effort expended. Commercial and other non-military methods were meeting their needs.

Even so it is open to question whether the British disengaged with sufficient rapidity from many regions east of Suez after 1956. The nation continued to bear an excessive military burden (compared with leading trading rivals), while cabinets into the 1960s seemed as intent upon the pursuit of influence in the world as in generating the means to sustain that influence. Extra-European preoccupations also distracted Britain from possible opportunities in Europe – or so many would argue. Suez, indeed, might seem a minor aberration, compared with the failure to join the EEC at its inception in 1957, while even the policy of close relations with the United States entailed costs as well as apparent advantages.[40] The private secretary to more than one Conservative prime minister claimed that, by the early 1960s, the United States – much more than British business interests or any other influence – was urging the British government to maintain a military presence east of Suez. Thus Denis Healey, minister of defence in the newly formed Wilson cabinet in 1964, returned from a visit to Washington to assure his colleagues that the Americans valued Britain's military role in the Indian Ocean more highly than her contribution to Nato. It is true that British governments had reasons of their own for perpetuating the east of Suez presence, but among them was the calculation that this was one of the best means whereby Britain could continue to exert influence in Washington. Both governments saw communism and radical nationalism as a threat to their interests in many lands bordering the Indian Ocean in the early and mid-1960s, even if in practice their priorities and perceptions did not always coincide.

One of the first notable critics of this presence east of Suez was the distinguished student of war, Liddell Hart. In 1960 he likened British bases in Aden and Singapore to 'crumbling sand castles' and insisted that British oil interests in the Middle East could best be defended by the adoption of the 'detached role of "the good customer"'. Yet in the run-up to the 1964 election the Conservatives seemed intent on acquiring a whole new generation of military hardware with the east of Suez role specifically in mind. De Gaulle's veto on British entry to the EEC in 1963 also strengthened anti-European feeling. The Labour Party waxed eloquent on the future of a multiracial Commonwealth led by Britain, India and Canada. The main difference between the Tories and Labour in office before and after 1964 was that the latter at first tried to pursue similar policies within a reduced arms budget. It was circumstances which forced policy reappraisals. A war between India and Pakistan was resolved by Soviet, not British mediation. Indonesian opposition to the British-inspired federation of Malaysia led to a 'Confrontation' in 1963–6 which, though only small-scale military action took place, necessitated a large British presence until a settlement was concluded. It was accepted in 1966 that the base in Aden was untenable in the face of local opposition. The Arab–Israeli war of 1967 demonstrated the vulnerability of British oil supplies from the Middle East despite a British military presence in the Persian Gulf. Britain's own economic problems were worsening, resulting in another devaluation in 1967 with extensive cuts in government spending. Labour's left wing refused to accept welfare economies without reductions to the armed forces. By then, however, the cabinet itself was already moving towards a rapid run-down in the British presence east of Suez. Advocates of withdrawal were even becoming active within the Conservative Party. Controversy over coloured immigration in Britain was lessening enthusiasm for the Commonwealth, while trade with members of the Commonwealth was in relative decline. Not surprisingly Conservative promises to reverse the trend of Labour policy came to little in the early 1970s, especially under a prime minister who was intent on entry to the EEC.

Declining interest in and enthusiasm for the Commonwealth, coupled with fears concerning the durability of the Anglo-American relationship in the 1960s, contributed to the British reappraisal of policies towards the European Economic Community which had been established in 1957. By the early 1960s Macmillan was convinced of the futility of efforts to remain outside and yet comfortably co-exist with and even shape the growth of the community in accordance with British interests. Even Britain's influence in the world and more specifically with the United States was under threat. He accordingly manoeuvred to win assent in Britain to an application for membership. In public he laid great stress on the supposed economic advantages of membership, but it is widely agreed that his prime motives were political – the maintenance and even enhancement of British influence both within Europe and with the United States.[41] Indeed, the economic pros and cons of membership were generally viewed as evenly matched within government at this time. Nevertheless the government could not carry the country with it without making a persuasive economic case, and without the support of powerful economic interest groups.[42]

At this stage, however, President de Gaulle of France insisted that Britain was too entangled with the Commonwealth and the United States for her to take on the role of a good European. He vetoed the first British application in 1963. If, as has been asserted, the Foreign Office was aware from the activities of British Intelligence that a veto was almost certain, the conclusion of the 1962 Polaris agreement with the United States and the haggling in favour of Commonwealth exports no longer appear to have been tactical errors. More than impressionistic answers, however, are impossible until the release of the relevant archival material in the early 1990s. Meanwhile experience of office from 1964 soon persuaded a majority of the Labour leaders that they too should make a bid for entry. Trade with the Commonwealth was not expanding in accordance with the estimates given in Labour's 1964 election propaganda. Indeed, a run of national economic crises was perhaps the major reason why the prime minister, Harold Wilson, now turned to the EEC. He needed to regain the political initiative at home, and here was also an opportunity to deny the Conservatives an issue at the next election.[43] But always there was the growing feeling in many influential quarters that only through membership could Britain reverse the decline in her international position. As a strong supporter of entry, Roy (Lord) Jenkins, later insisted, 'an effective leadership role in the Community . . . was not the least of the reasons why we joined'.[44] Some supporters of the EEC shared the sensation recorded by Anthony Sampson in 1965 that 'to visit the capitals of the Common Market is to see how much the new sense of mobility and opportunity, and the awareness of competitive neighbours, can help to bring new vigour to old countries'.[45] A pro-entry House of Commons vote of no less than 488 to 62 in 1967 nevertheless failed to persuade de Gaulle that he should reverse his earlier veto.

Opinion in Britain concerning the EEC was also highly unstable, as the domestic trials of the next Conservative government under Edward Heath demonstrated. A majority in the Labour Party speedily asserted itself against the proposed terms of entry. Dissidents also existed in Conservative ranks, thus necessitating a free parliamentary vote on the issue in October 1971. Despite Britain's formal entry in 1973, her membership remained in doubt until another Labour government had renegotiated some of the terms of entry and had submitted the question to the public in 1975 in the form of a referendum. In the 1970s the EEC was a domestic rather than a foreign political question, with the left asserting itself in the Labour Party and presenting it as a struggle between socialism and capitalism. Not surprisingly a somewhat bemused electorate, faced by party divisions and the esoteric nature of the issues, appeared to respond in the 1975 referendum mainly in accordance with the alignment of the leading personalities on either side. In the end Harold Wilson, James Callaghan, Edward Heath and Jeremy Thorpe (the Liberal leader) comfortably outweighed Tony Benn, Michael Foot and Enoch Powell.

James Callaghan, the minister responsible for renegotiation in 1974–5, concludes in his memoirs that only through membership of the EEC could Britain exercise significant influence in the world.[46] At the same time he recalls that during the renegotiation process he often felt that he was filling the role of 'not so much a Foreign Secretary as a multiple grocer', given the mundane character of the issues under discussion. Nor did the EEC seem capable of rising to higher matters thereafter, as agricultural and other forms of overproduction dominated its agenda. In the eyes of the British public it was famed for its bureaucracy, its rigidities, and internal rows rather than for its earlier dynamism. The economic advantages for Britain fell short of those promised during the long debate leading up to 1975. In the 1980s, to the dismay of EEC enthusiasts who were looking for more positive action, Mrs Thatcher earned political dividends at home with her highly publicised campaigns to cut Britain's financial contribution, to execute a thorough reform of the community's finances, and to reduce its notorious farming surpluses. Of all the Community's peoples the British were perhaps the least committed.[47]

In these circumstances it was not surprising that British entry to the EEC was soon followed by renewed British emphasis on trans-Atlantic ties. These were particularly important in all that related to defence. Early in the Conservative administration of Mrs Thatcher (from 1979) agreement was reached on the purchase of American Trident missiles to replace Polaris in the 1990s. The British also received vital intelligence and military equipment from the United States during the 1982 conflict with Argentina over the Falkland Islands. It is true that by the later 1980s, as questions were once again being asked about the strength of the long-term American commitment to the defence of Europe, so there was renewed interest in closer British military co-operation with the leading Western European states. Yet even in the 1980s British foreign and defence policies continued to bear some resemblance to those developed in the early post-war period. The British were still, in many ways, the offshore island-ers of Europe, and as such alive to any opportunity to exert influence over or to draw support from the United States. British foreign policy continued to retain many links with past habits and attitudes.

# CONCLUSIONS

THE WORDS 'Decline', 'Retreat' and 'Crisis' appear regularly in the titles and in the body of studies of British foreign policy in the twentieth century. Bernard Porter lugubriously writes of a 'diplomatic revolution' which has interrupted Britain's natural pattern of development, leaving Britain increasingly exposed to the influence of other powers. Entries into both Nato and the EEC are seen as departures from the 'old wisdom', a retreat from the traditional independent role and from a worldwide international vision. His reluctant verdict is that by the second half of the twentieth century the 'best good was simply not attainable any more'.[1] Paul Kennedy is rather less fatalistic, and sees scope for criticism of the British leadership from 1945, and especially from the 1960s. It was more indecisive than that of powers of comparable rank because 'to a large extent . . . the leaders were no longer clear where they were going'.[2] In the view of Roy Douglas Britain's last opportunity to arrest or delay her decline occurred when she decided to fight Germany in September 1939.[3]

A much more philosophical verdict was offered by W. N. Medlicott in 1967. He emphasised the unusual circumstances in Britain, Europe and the world which made possible the era of Britain's ascendancy and her consequent ability during much of the nineteenth century to steer clear of major wars or deep involvement in the European continent. He argued that 'the

122

story of British foreign policy since the beginning of the [twenti-eth] century should not be regarded as one of shrinking power or a shrinking from the use of power but rather a long process of adaptation to the realities of the modern world.' As if inspired by the shade of the third Marquess of Salisbury he went on: 'There was perhaps no particular disadvantage [in the late 1960s] in allowing international affairs to follow their own course for the time being, and no particular evidence that any initiative on her part at this stage would usefully divert the tide of events.'[4] Britain, he implied, needed to develop the outlook of a second-rank state which did not think in terms of leadership or a predominant role, but which might nevertheless improve its international position through realistic calculation and skilful, if unheroic diplomacy.

Adaptation, however, may be essentially reactive or positive in character, and well into the second half of the twentieth century British policy-makers often seemed happier responding to events rather than essaying bold initiatives. In the process they frequently discovered that the outcomes which they wished to avoid had been forced upon them. Both the policies of entente and appeasement were intended to avert war. After 1945 Britain largely turned her back on Europe for as long as she dared, and when at last she turned to the EEC it was with a marked lack of enthusiasm. If one were to use the criteria of those in power at the start of the century, British foreign policy over the next three generations must be adjudged a failure. Even for those prepared to accept that some change was inevitable, it had occurred at a disconcertingly rapid pace and on an undesirable scale.

Yet of the importance of British policy-making – at least until the 1960s – foreign practitioners of power politics had few doubts whether their verdicts were critical or favourable. Indeed the German leadership before 1918, and the Americans until the 1950s probably credited the British with influence and cunning beyond their deserts, the one accusing the British of a policy of encirclement and the others fearing manipulation of American power to the advantage of Great Britain. The British were also influential in what they did not do – from their failure to act vigorously in Europe between the wars to their refusal to follow a Europe-first policy in the late 1940s and during the 1950s. So delicately interconnected was the chain of causation, and so keen the attention directed by other capitals to thinking in London, that the microscopic analysis to which so much of British policy in this century has been subjected seems amply justified. British policy, even at its most cautious and defensive, and whatever the reality of British power, continued to matter. Nor was Britain alone among the great powers in this century in reaching an unscheduled destination by unexpected routes.

It might also be argued that, in practice, Britain's fortunes and prospects have not necessarily changed for the worse since 1900. The superpowers have not always found life at the top a comfortable or rewarding experience. Britain's relatively disappointing economic performance has not been due to the loss of her position as a world power – indeed, her determination to act as a leading and an imperial power has often compounded her economic problems, especially from 1945. On the other hand, in the period following the Second World War it might be argued, depending upon one's point of view, that the developed non-communist world has so far tended to evolve on lines more in accord with British interests than at any time since the 1900s. In some respects, therefore, Britain has benefited from the creation of a new international environment despite her own policy-makers.

In an era of such turbulence and change, success and even survival were dependent upon generous slices of luck. Indeed, so strange have been many of the twists in the history of this century that more intelligent long-term planning might have served the British no better than their own pragmatic approach. Nevertheless, understandable though it is given their experience of the world in the preceding 200 years, their efforts to minimise the effects of change upon long-established British interests and ways of doing things meant that at several critical moments their policies were either overtaken or seemed in danger of being overtaken by events – from the ententes, through appeasement to Churchill's 'three circles'. As it happened the British were blessed with not a little good fortune – even if this was not always apparent at the time. They were reprieved in spite of their policies. Granted extra time they were able to make adjustments less painfully than some other imperial nations. Furthermore, even when obviously muddling through, or reacting late in the day, the British were at times able to vindicate their own confidence in their knowledge of the world and expertise in international statecraft.

# NOTES

## INTRODUCTION

1. K. Wilson (ed.), *British Foreign Secretaries: from the Crimean War to the First World War* (London, 1987), p. 19.
2. A. Sampson, *The Anatomy of Britain* (London, 1962), pp. 624–8.
3. See Christopher Thorne in *The English Historical Review* (1977), pp. 827ff.; K. Bourne, *Britain and the Balance of Power in North America, 1815–1908* (London, 1967), p. 350. Douglas Hurd, *An End to Promises* (London, 1979), pp. 58–64, praises Edward Heath for transcending the anti-French bias of the Foreign Office in the negotiations leading to British entry to the EEC in the early 1970s.
4. See A. Porter in Lord Blake and R. Cecil (eds), *Salisbury: the Man and his Policies* (London, 1987), pp. 155–9.

## 1. PARTIAL COMMITMENT AND TOTAL WAR

1. Blake and Cecil (eds), *Salisbury*, p. 171.
2. B. Semmell, *Liberalism and Naval Strategy* (London, 1986), p. 176.
3. For a full discussion of these themes, see B. Porter, *Britain, Europe and the World, 1850–1982* (London, 1982).
4. Blake and Cecil (eds), *Salisbury*, p. 176.
5. D. French, *The British Economy and Strategic Planning, 1905–15* (London, 1982), pp. 17–19, 30–6, 51–7, 85.
6. The importance of *weltpolitik* is emphasised by I. Geiss, *German Foreign Policy, 1871–1914* (London, 1976), pp. viii, 22, 84, 96, etc.
7. I. Nish, *The Anglo-Japanese Alliance, 1894–1907* (London, 1966), pp. 243–4.
8. See D. Gillard in Wilson, *British Foreign Secretaries*, p. 135, for a further defence of Salisbury.
9. Nish, *Anglo-Japanese Alliance*, p. 376.
10. Compare ibid., pp. 286–7 and G. Monger, *The End of Isolation* (London, 1963), chapters 6 and 7.
11. K. Wilson, *The Policy of Entente* (Cambridge, 1985), p. 71.

12. J. A. S. Grenville, *Lord Salisbury and Foreign Policy at the Close of the Nineteenth Century* (London, 1970), p. 44.
13. Z. S. Steiner, *Britain and the Origins of the First World War* (London, 1977), p. 33; S. R. Williamson, *The Politics of Grand Strategy: Britain and France Prepare for War, 1904–1914* (Cambridge, Mass., 1969), pp. 14–16.
14. Monger, *End of Isolation*, pp. 158–9. On Lansdowne see P. J. V. Rolo in Wilson, *British Foreign Secretaries*, chapter 6.
15. Williamson, *Politics of Grand Strategy*, p. 250.
16. Porter, *Britain, Europe and the World*, pp. 76, 81. Compare the verdicts on Grey of K. Robbins, *Sir Edward Grey* (London, 1971), p. 372, and K. Wilson, *British Foreign Secretaries*, pp. 191–2.
17. Monger, *End of Isolation*, p. 281.
18. Steiner, *Britain*, p. 83.
19. Wilson, *Policy of Entente*, p. 75.
20. Wilson, *British Foreign Secretaries*, pp. 177–87.
21. Wilson, *Policy of Entente*, p. 74. G. P. Gooch and H. W. V. Temperley (eds), *British Documents on the Origins of the War, 1898–1914* (London, 1926–38), iii, 266–77.
22. Gooch and Temperley, *British Documents*, iii, 389–40. Note also Williamson, *Politics of Grand Strategy*, p. 103.
23. Gooch and Temperley, *British Documents*, vi, 108, 117, 266, 279.
24. D. Dilks (ed.), *Retreat from Power* (London, 1981), i, 6. Monger, *End of Isolation*, p. 327.
25. Steiner, *Britain*, pp. 42, 78.
26. Gooch and Temperley, *British Documents*, iii, 415, 417, 418.
27. Wilson, *Policy of Entente*, pp. 77–8.
28. Ibid., chapters 4 and 6.
29. Gooch and Temperley, *British Documents*, vi, 261; xi, 121.
30. Ibid., vi, 738–9.
31. See K. Wilson in Dilks (ed.), *Retreat from Power*, i, 38, 40.
32. D. Gillard, *The Struggle for Asia, 1828–1914* (London, 1977), p. 178.
33. M. Howard, *The Continental Commitment* (London, 1972), p. 29.
34. See P. Schroeder in D. E. Lee (ed.), *The Outbreak of the First World War* (Lexington, 1975), pp. 148–69.
35. See J. Grenville in D. Read (ed.), *Edwardian England* (London, 1982), pp. 162–80.
36. A. Marwick, *The Century of Total War* (Oxford, 1968), p. 47. See also A. J. Mayer, *The Persistence of the Old Regime* (London, 1981).
37. J. Joll, *The Origins of the First World War* (London, 1984), pp. 95–8. See also C. Nicolson in A. O'Day (ed.), *The Edwardian Age* (London, 1979), chapter 8, especially pp. 163ff., and A. J. A. Morris, *The Scaremongers, 1896–1914* (London, 1984).
38. Steiner, *Britain*, pp. 149–51.
39. R. C. K. Ensor, *England 1870–1914* (Oxford, 1949), p. 575. See C. Nicolson in O'Day (ed.), *Edwardian Age*, pp. 155–6, and M. Schwartz in A. J. A. Morris (ed.), *Edwardian Radicalism* (London, 1974), pp. 258–9.
40. Compare the more critical view of Grey adopted by Steiner, *Britain*, p. 127 with Robbins, *Sir Edward Grey*, p. 372.
41. For British war aims see D. Stevenson, *The First World War and International Relations* (Oxford, 1988), *passim*; J. Gooch, *The Prospect of War* (London,

1981), pp. 127ff.; and J. Grigg, *Lloyd George: from peace to war* (London, 1985), pp. 419–20.

42. D. C. Watt, *Succeeding John Bull* (Cambridge, 1984), pp. 31–6.

43. M. Beloff, *Imperial Sunset: Britain's liberal empire, 1897–1921* (London, 1969), p. 184.

44. C. Barnett, *The Collapse of British Power* (London, 1972), p. 318.

45. See S. Marks in G. Martel (ed.), *The Origins of the Second World War Reconsidered* (London, 1986), chapter 1, and Gooch, *Prospect of War*, pp. 141–2.

46. D. Stevenson, *French War Aims against Germany, 1914–1919* (Oxford, 1982), pp. 212–14.

47. P. Kennedy, *The Realities behind Diplomacy* (London, 1981), pp. 220, 225.

48. See, e.g., D. C. Watt, *Personalities and Policies* (London, 1965), p. 30.

49. L. Jaffe, *The Decision to Disarm Germany* (London, 1985), pp. 195–207.

50. A. Lentin, *Guilt at Versailles* (London, 1985), pp. 121, 131.

51. H. Nicolson, *Peacemaking 1919* (London, 1964), pp. 91, 101, 207–9.

52. W. N. Medlicott, *British Foreign Policy Since Versailles* (London, 1968), p. 3. K. O. Morgan, *Consensus and Disunity: the Lloyd George coalition government, 1918–22* (Oxford, 1979), especially chapter 5.

53. H. I. Nelson, *Land and Power: British and allied policy on Germany's frontiers, 1916–19* (London, 1963), pp. 366–70.

54. F. S. Northedge, *The Troubled Giant* (London, 1966), pp. 122–4.

55. R. H. Ullman, *Anglo-Soviet Relations, 1917–21* (Princeton, 1973), iii, 467, 473. On government fears of labour unrest, see Marwick, *Century of Total War*, pp. 146–65.

## 2. TOO MANY CHALLENGES

1. A. J. P. Taylor, *English History, 1914–45* (Oxford, 1965), pp. 221–2.

2. K. Middlemas and J. Barnes, *Baldwin: a biography* (London, 1969), p. 285; see also pp. 225, 327.

3. Ibid., p. 341; Barnett, *Collapse of British Power*, pp. 275, 278; H. Nicolson, *King George V* (London, 1952), pp. 405, 407.

4. K. Bourne and D. C. Watt (eds), *British Documents on Foreign Affairs: reports and papers from the Foreign Office confidential print: the Soviet Union, 1917–1939* (University Publications of America, 1986), vol. 8, p. 187.

5. Medlicott, *British Foreign Policy*, p. 31. M. Cowling, *The Impact of Hitler* (London, 1975), p. 397. Barnett, *Collapse of British Power*, pp. 272–7.

6. I. Nish, *Alliance in Decline, 1908–23* (London, 1972), p. 392.

7. W. R. Louis, *British Strategy in the Far East, 1919–39* (Oxford, 1971), p. 46. *Documents on British Foreign Policy, 1919–39*, ed. E. L. Woodward *et al.* (London, 1947 continuing), 1st series, iii, 725–32, etc.

8. See S. Marks in Martel, *Origins . . . Reconsidered*, pp. 32–5; A. Orde, *Great Britain and International Security* (London, 1978), pp. 211–12; B. Bond, *British Military Policy between Two World Wars* (Oxford, 1980), pp. 79–94.

9. W. J. Mommsen and L. Kettenacher (eds), *The Fascist Challenge and the Policy of Appeasement* (London, 1983), p. 103.

10. A. Adamthwaite, *The Making of the Second World War* (London, 1977), p. 52.

11. A. R. Peters, *Anthony Eden at the Foreign Office, 1931–8* (Aldershot, 1986), p. 186.

12. See P. Kennedy in Martel, *Origins . . . Reconsidered*, p. 155, and his review article in *The Times Higher Education Supplement*, 20 March 1987.
13. F. S. Northedge, *The Troubled Giant: Britain among the Great Powers, 1916–39* (London, 1966), pp. 618–19. A. J. P. Taylor, *The Origins of the Second World War* (London, 1961), p. 189.
14. M. Gilbert, *The Roots of Appeasement* (London, 1966), p. xii; Howard, *Continental Commitment*, pp. 100–2.
15. Barnett, *Collapse of British Power*, pp. 24–43, etc.; Kennedy, *Realities*, pp. 253–7.
16. Kennedy, *Realities*, p. 301.
17. Northedge, *Troubled Giant*, p. 272; Kennedy, *Realities*, p. 256.
18. S. Roskill, *Hankey: Man of Secrets* (London, 1972), ii, 544–5.
19. Compare Porter, *Britain, Europe and the World*, pp. 95–6, and Kennedy, *Realities*, pp. 257, 301.
20. See G. C. Peden, *British Rearmament and the Treasury* (Edinburgh, 1979), and G. Schmidt, *The Politics and Economics of Appeasement* (Leamington Spa, 1986), *passim*.
21. W. Wark, *The Ultimate Enemy: British Intelligence and Nazi Germany* (London, 1985), pp. 205–10; Williamson Murray, *The Change in the European Balance of Power* (Princeton, 1984), pp. 62–8, 157–61, 208–10, 218–63, 285.
22. *Documents on British Foreign Policy*, series 3, ii, 490.
23. A. J. P. Taylor, *The Trouble Makers* (London, 1957), pp. 185–99; J. F. Naylor, *Labour's International Policy* (London, 1969), pp. 252ff.; P. Williams, *Hugh Gaitskell* (London, 1979), p. 86.
24. K. Hildebrand, *The Foreign Policy of the Third Reich* (London, 1973), pp. 54–5. See also Kennedy, *Realities*, p. 301.
25. *Foreign Relations of the United States* (FRUS), (Washington, 1938), i, 632. G. Hagglof, *Diplomat* (Stockholm, 1971), p. 103.
26. D. Dilks (ed.), *The Diaries of Sir Alexander Cadogan* (London, 1971), p. 119.
27. A. A. Gromyko (ed.), *Soviet Foreign Policy, 1917–45* (Moscow, 1981). See also F. S. Northedge and A. Wells, *Britain and Soviet Communism* (London, 1982), p. 65.
28. Dilks, *Retreat from Power*, i, 145.
29. Bourne and Watt, *British Documents*, vol. 14, p. 436.
30. B. Bond, *Chief of Staff: the diaries of Sir Henry Pownall* (London, 1972), i, 174. See also pp. 175, 193 for Pownall's fears that war with Germany was inevitable, though not necessarily over Eastern Europe, and that German 'peaceful' penetration of the Balkans would be acceptable.
31. *Documents on British Foreign Policy*, series 3, iii, 525. See D. C. Watt in M. Bentley and J. Stevenson (eds), *High and Low Politics in Modern Britain* (Oxford, 1983), chapter 8, especially pp. 239–40.
32. Dilks, *Retreat from Power*, i, 145–6.
33. J. Haslam, *The Soviet Union and the Struggle for Collective Security in Europe, 1933–9* (London, 1984), p. 194.
34. S. Newman, *March 1939* (Oxford, 1976), *passim*.
35. G. C. Peden, 'A Matter of Timing: the economic background to British foreign policy, 1937–9', *History*, 69 (1984), 19–20.
36. M. Gilbert, *Winston S. Churchill*, vol. 5, *Companion* Part 3 (London, 1982), pp. 1374, 1573, 1580.
37. D. Carlton, *Anthony Eden* (London, 1981), pp. 147–50.
38. Cowling, *Impact of Hitler*, p. 9; Wark, *Ultimate Enemy*, pp. 219–20; D. C.

Watt in Bentley and Stevenson (eds), *High and Low Politics*, pp. 225–38; Newman, *March 1939*, pp. 96–104.

39. A. J. Prazmowska, 'War over Danzig? The Dilemma of Anglo-Polish Relations in the Months preceding the Outbreak of the Second World War', *Historical Journal*, 26 (1983), 177–8.
40. W. S. Churchill, *The Gathering Storm* (London, 1948), p. 272.
41. Northedge and Wells, *Britain and Soviet Communism*, pp. 67–8; Wark, *Ultimate Enemy*, pp. 213–22.
42. G. L. Weinberg, *The Foreign Policy of Hitler's Germany, 1937–9* (Chicago, 1980), pp. 503–14, 533–4, 551–2, 575–7, 580–1.
43. Gromyko, *Soviet Foreign Policy*, pp. 368–77. See also note 33 above.
44. For the Anglo-Soviet talks, see *Soviet Peace Efforts on the Eve of World War II* (Moscow, 1973), *passim*; S. Aster, *The Making of the Second World War* (London, 1973), *passim*; Bentley and Stevenson (eds), *High and Low Politics*, pp. 238–54.
45. *Documents on British Foreign Policy*, series 3, vii, 354n.
46. Cowling, *Impact of Hitler*, pp. 9, 12. R. Douglas, *World Crisis and British Decline* (London, 1986), p. 94. See Taylor, *English History*, p. 453, for stress on the influence of the House of Commons.
47. Barnett, *Collapse of British Power*, pp. 574–5.
48. P. M. H. Bell, *The Origins of the Second World War in Europe* (London, 1986), p. 181.

## 3. FROM WORLD WAR TO COLD WAR

1. Lord Gladwyn, *The Memoirs of Lord Gladwyn* (London, 1972), chapter 8.
2. V. Rothwell, *Britain in the Cold War, 1941–7* (London, 1982), pp. 2–3.
3. Ibid., p. 15.
4. Ibid., p. 134.
5. V. Mastny, *Russia's Road to the Cold War* (New York, 1979), pp. 309–10. M. Kitchen, 'Winston Churchill and the Soviet Union during the Second World War', *Historical Journal*, 30 (1987), 415–36.
6. Anthony Glees, *The Secrets of the Service* (London, 1987), *passim*.
7. B. Arcidiacono, 'The "Dress Rehearsal": the Foreign Office and the Control of Italy, 1943–4', *Historical Journal*, 28 (1985), 417–27.
8. Rothwell, *Britain in the Cold War*, pp. 118–23.
9. G. Ross, *The Foreign Office and the Kremlin. British documents on Anglo-Soviet Relations, 1941–5* (Cambridge, 1984), pp. 146, 165, 173ff., 183ff., 193–9; L. Kettenacker, 'The Anglo-Soviet alliance and the problem of Germany, 1941–5', *Journal of Contemporary History*, 17 (1982), 440–5, 446–54; Rothwell, *Britain in the Cold War*, p. 127.
10. G. Ross, 'Foreign Office Attitudes to the Soviet Union, 1941–5', *Journal of Contemporary History*, 16 (1981), 521–40. See also Ross, *Foreign Office and the Kremlin*, pp. 218–23, and Rothwell, *Britain in the Cold War*, pp. 115–93.
11. M. Howard, *The Mediterranean Strategy in the Second World War* (London, 1968), *passim*; E. Barker, *British Policy in South-East Europe in the Second World War* (London, 1976), especially pp. 123–5.
12. See H. B. Ryan, 'A New Look at Churchill's "Iron Curtain" Speech', *Historical Journal*, 22 (1979), 895–920, for the suggestion that Labour's initial strategy towards the USSR was closer to that of Roosevelt than

Churchill. See also K. O. Morgan, *Labour in Power, 1945–51* (Oxford, 1984), pp. 235–6.

13. A. Bullock, *Ernest Bevin: foreign secretary, 1945–51* (London, 1983), pp. 116–18, 199, 214–17.

14. See below, notes 18–19.

15. See G. C. Peden in J. Becker and F. Knipping (eds), *Power in Europe? Great Britain, France, Italy and Germany in a Postwar World* (Berlin and New York, 1986), pp. 248–9.

16. For recent scholarly criticism of the British decision to accept the American loan see B. Pimlott, *Hugh Dalton* (London, 1985), pp. 480–520; also R.Bullen and M. E. Pelly (eds), *Documents on British Policy Overseas* (HMSO, 1986), series 1, vol. 3, pp. xxiv, 310–13, 400–1, etc.

17. See, e.g., E. Barker, *The British between the Superpowers, 1945–50* (London, 1983), *passim*.

18. Bullock, *Ernest Bevin*, pp. 353–4.

19. The best brief treatment is by R. Smith and J. Zametica, 'The Cold Warrior: Clement Attlee Reconsidered, 1945–7', *International Affairs*, 61 (Spring, 1985), 237–51.

20. For Montgomery's frequently strained relations with the other chiefs of staff, see J. Clarke, *Templer: Tiger of Malaya* (London, 1986), pp. 174–5.

21. Pimlot, *Hugh Dalton*, pp 480–520.

22. Bevin to the Overseas Reconstruction Committee, 18 June 1946, FO371/55588. I am indebted to Mr Alan Richer for this reference.

23. D. Dilks in O. Riste (ed.), *Western Security: the formative years, 1947–53* (Oslo, 1985), p. 44.

24. Clarke, *Templer*, p. 172.

25. Rothwell, *Britain in the Cold War*, p. 434. R. Frazier, 'Did Britain start the Cold War? Bevin and the Truman Doctrine', *Historical Journal*, 27 (1984), 715–27.

26. Watt, *Succeeding John Bull*, p. 119.

27. For a review of this controversy see J. Melissen and Bert Zeeman, 'Britain and Western Europe, 1945–51: opportunities lost?', *International Affairs*, 63 (Winter, 1986–7), 81–95. Note also Sean Greenwood, 'Ernest Bevin, France and "Western Union": August 1945–February 1946', *European History Quarterly*, 14 (July 1984), 319–38.

28. J. W. Young, *Britain, France and the Unity of Europe, 1945–51* (Leicester, 1984), *passim*.

29. Allister E. Hinds, 'Sterling and Imperial Preference, 1945–51', *Journal of Imperial and Commonwealth History*, 15 (1987), 148–69.

30. See G. C. Peden in Becker and Knipping (eds), *Power in Europe*, pp. 256–60.

31. A. Adamthwaite, 'Britain in the World, 1945–9: the view from the Foreign Office', *International Affairs*, 61 (Spring 1985), 223–35.

32. A. S. Milward, *The Reconstruction of Western Europe, 1945–51* (London, 1984), pp. 343–61.

33. H. Pelling, *The Labour Governments, 1945–51* (London, 1984), p. 145; Morgan, *Labour in Power*, p. 275.

34. G. Warner in O. Riste (ed.), *Western Security*, p. 263.

35. Barker, *The British between the Superpowers*, pp. 111, 175–85.

36. See e.g. V. Rothwell in R. Crockatt and S. Smith (eds), *The Cold War Past and Present* (London, 1987), pp. 72–4.

37. J. Schneer, 'Hopes Deferred or Shattered: the British Labour Left and the Third Force Movement, 1945–9', *Journal of Modern History*, 56 (1984), 197–226. See also Northedge and Wells, *Britain and Soviet Communism*, pp. 122–4.

38. See British Cabinet Papers and Memoranda, CAB 129/29 CP(48)223.

39. N. Petersen, 'Bargaining power among potential allies: negotiating the North Atlantic Treaty, 1948–9', *Review of International Studies*, 12 (July 1986), 187–203.

40. N. Hamilton, *Monty: the Field Marshal, 1944–76* (London, 1986), p. 773.

41. Barker, *The British between the Superpowers*, pp. 120–62.

42. R. Ovendale, *The English-Speaking Alliance, 1945–51* (London, 1985), chapter 6.

43. Ibid., pp. 218–20.

44. CAB129/43 CP(50) 294.

45. CAB129/44 CP(51) 16, 20.

46. R. Foot, *The Wrong War: American Policy and the Dimensions of the Korean Conflict, 1950–53* (Ithaca and London, 1985), especially p. 243.

47. S. Duke, *United States Defence Bases in the United Kingdom* (London, 1987), pp. 64–8. I am also indebted to Dr David Gates of the Centre for Defence Studies, University of Aberdeen, for guidance on this question.

48. Duke, *US Defence Bases*, pp. 70–2.

49. Bullock, *Ernest Bevin*, pp. 101, 104, 843–7. Barker, *The British between the Superpowers*, p. 242.

50. See Rothwell in Crockatt and Smith (eds), *Cold War*, pp. 64–73.

51. Ibid., pp. 64ff. See also a review by K. O. Morgan in *English Historical Review*, 152 (1987), 761–2. Barker, *The British between the Superpowers*, p. 241.

52. Bullock, *Ernest Bevin*, p. 841.

## 4. REAPPRAISALS AND READJUSTMENTS

1. CAB 129/52 CP(52) 172–3.

2. CAB 129/52 C(52)202; see also CAB 129/54 C(52) 253. For an analysis of British policy in this period see A. Adamthwaite, 'Overstretched and overstrung: Eden, the Foreign Office and the making of policy, 1951–55', *International Affairs*, 64 (1988), 241–59.

3. Treasury memorandum of 28 November 1955, CAB 129/78 CP(55) 184. For earlier fears see the chancellor's memo. of 24 July 1953, CAB 129/62 C(53) 211.

4. CAB 129/54 C(54)329. For the evolution of British nuclear thinking see especially Peter Malone, *The British Nuclear Deterrent* (London, 1984).

5. M. M. Gowing, *Independence and Deterrence: Britain and atomic energy, 1945–52* (London, 1974), i, 441. Duke, *US Defence Bases*, p. 103.

6. FRUS (1952–4), vol. vi, part 1, pp. 695–717, especially pp. 709–10.

7. H. Kissinger, *The White House Years* (London, 1979), pp. 90–1. See also *The Years of Upheaval* (London, 1982).

8. CAB 129/74 C(55) 95.

9. Duke, *US Defence Bases*, p. 128; Malone, *British Nuclear Deterrent*, pp. 31, 87–90.

10. J. Frankel, *British Foreign Policy, 1945–73* (London, 1975), p. 306.

11. H. G. Nicholas, *The United States and Britain* (London, 1975), p. 129. The

pros and cons of British strategy are usefully and concisely discussed by J. Baylis, *Anglo-American Defence Relations, 1939–84* (London, 1984), especially chapter 8. See also A. J. R. Groom, *British Thinking about Nuclear Weapons* (London, 1974). For early insights into Labour's controversies over nuclear weapons see J. Morgan (ed.), *The Backbench Diaries of Richard Crossman* (London, 1981), pp. 385–90, 396–7.

12. Groom, *British Thinking*, pp. 566–7.

13. Cited in *The Times*, 2 January 1985. See also Duke, *US Defence Bases*, p. 106.

14. *The Times*, 2 January 1984. Groom, *British Thinking*, p. 63.

15. Sir David Hunt, *On the Spot* (London, 1975), p. 56. See *The Times*, 3 January 1985, for the objections of Lord Salisbury.

16. Carlton, *Anthony Eden*, p. 339.

17. Cited in *The Times*, 3 January 1985.

18. J. Cable, *The Geneva Conference and Indo-China* (London, 1986), p. 300.

19. CAB 129/54 C(54) 263 and 271. See J. L. Gaddis, *Strategies of Containment* (London, 1982), p. 149n. for Eisenhower's temporary refusal to rule out all thought of a preventive war.

20. R. Boardman, *Britain and the People's Republic of China, 1949–74* (London, 1976), pp. 65–76.

21. Sir W. Hayter, *A Double Life* (London, 1974), pp. 120–4, 151–2.

22. CAB 129/74 C(55) 83; 129/76 C(55) 99.

23. A. Buchan and P. Windsor, *Arms and Stability in Europe* (London, 1963), pp. 43–5; see also D. C. Watt in K. Kaiser and R. Morgan, *Britain and West Germany* (London, 1971), chapter 11.

24. G. T. Seaborg, *Kennedy, Khruschchev and the Test Ban* (Berkeley and London, 1981), p. 113.

25. A. M. Schlesinger, *A Thousand Days: J. F. Kennedy in the White House* (London, 1965), pp. 433, 762, 765.

26. Ibid., pp. 379, 699ff.

27. C. J. Bartlett, *A History of Postwar Britain* (London, 1977), p. 121.

28. Dean Acheson, *Present at the Creation* (London, 1970), p. 600.

29. Eden to the cabinet, 11 February 1952, CAB 129/52 CP(52) 32.

30. Eden to the cabinet, 16 February 1953, CAB 129/59 C(53) 65. P. Darby, *British Defence Policy East of Suez, 1947–68* (London, 1973), p. 47.

31. Darby, *Defence East of Suez*, pp. 66–7; E. Monroe, *Britain's Moment in the Middle East* (London, 1963), p. 183.

32. R. R. James, *Anthony Eden* (London, 1986), p. 399; Eden to the cabinet, 14 March 1955, CAB 129/74 C(55) 70.

33. James, *Anthony Eden*, pp. 490, 532–8, 592–3. For cabinet deliberations see J. Barnes in P. Hennessy and A. Seldon (eds), *Ruling Performance* (Oxford, 1987), pp. 112–15; P. Hennessy and M. Laity, 'Suez', *Contemporary Record*, 1 (1987), 5–6.

34. Macmillan to the cabinet, 13 October 1955, CAB 129/78 CP(55) 152.

35. Cited in *The Times*, 3 January 1987.

36. Ibid. Harold Macmillan, *Memoirs, 1914–63* (London, 1966–73), iv, chapter 4. See Hennessy and Laity, 'Suez', pp. 2–8, and Hennessy and Seldon, *Ruling Performance*, pp. 112–15, for analyses of recently released official documentation.

37. Hennessy and Laity, 'Suez', pp. 2–3.

38. J. Morgan, *Crossman Diaries*, pp. 517, 544–66.

39. Cited in *The Times*, 2 January 1988.

40. For an assessment of the disadvantages in the special relationship see Watt, *Succeeding John Bull*, and his chapter (4) in W. R. Louis and H. Bull (eds), *The Special Relationship: Anglo-American Relations since 1945* (Oxford, 1986). The pros and cons of a more positive British policy on Europe in the period 1955–8 are discussed by John Barnes in Hennessy and Seldon, *Ruling Performance*, pp. 130–2. Very few in Britain were conscious of a missed opportunity, though it is tempting to argue that a strong British lead might have produced a more broadly based and outward looking European grouping.

41. A. Sked and C. Cook, *Postwar Britain* (London, 1979), pp. 189–91; R. Lieber, *British Politics and European Unity* (Berkeley, 1970), p. 163. See also Kaiser and Morgan, *Britain and W. Germany*, pp. 173–4, and M. Pinto-Duschinsky in Hennessy and Seldon, *Ruling Performance*, pp. 162–5.

42. J. Baker, *Who Makes British Foreign Policy?* (Milton Keynes, 1976), pp. 68–9.

43. L. J. Robins, *The Reluctant Party: Labour and the EEC* (Ormskirk, 1979), pp. 61–119.

44. *The Times*, 30 January 1988.

45. A. Sampson, *The Anatomy of Britain Today* (London, 1965), p. 679.

46. J. Callaghan, *Time and Chance* (London, 1987), p. 305.

47. See, for instance, a MORI poll, *The Times*, 6 January 1988.

## CONCLUSIONS

1. Porter, *Britain, Europe and the World*, pp. 11, 127, 147.

2. Kennedy, *Realities*, pp. 379, 383ff.

3. Douglas, *World Crisis*, p. 271.

4. Medlicott, *British Foreign Policy*, p. 332.

# BIBLIOGRAPHY

This highly selective list of books and articles is intended to serve as a guide to further reading for students and undergraduates.

## BOOKS

Aster, S., *The Making of the Second World War* (London, 1973).

Baker, J., *Who Makes British Foreign Policy?* (Milton Keynes, 1976).

Barker, E., *Churchill and Eden at War* (London, 1978).

Barker, E., *British Policy in South-East Europe in the Second World War* (London, 1976).

Barker, E., *The British between the Superpowers, 1945–50* (London, 1983).

Baylis, J., *Anglo-American Defence Relations, 1939–84* (London, 1984).

Becker, J. and Knipping F. (eds), *Power in Europe? Great Britain, France, Italy and Germany in a Postwar World* (Berlin and New York, 1986).

Bond, B., *British Military Policy between Two World Wars* (Oxford, 1980).

Bullock, A., *Ernest Bevin: foreign secretary, 1945–51* (London, 1983).

Burridge, T., *Clement Attlee* (London, 1985).

Carlton, D., *Anthony Eden* (London, 1981).

Crockatt, R. and Smith, S. (eds), *The Cold War Past and Present* (London, 1987).

Darby, P., *British Defence Policy East of Suez, 1947–68* (Oxford, 1973).

Dilks, D., *Retreat from Power: studies in Britain's foreign policy of the twentieth century*, 2 vols (London, 1981).

Dockrill, M. L. and Goold, J. D., *Peace without Promise: Britain and the Peace Conferences, 1919–23* (London, 1981).

Douglas, R., *In the Year of Munich* (London, 1977).

Douglas, R., *The Advent of War, 1939–40* (London, 1978).

Douglas, R., *From War to Cold War, 1942–8* (London, 1981).

Douglas, R., *World Crisis and British Decline, 1929–56* (London, 1986).

Edmonds, R., *Setting the Mould: the United States and Britain, 1945–50* (Oxford, 1986).

Gilbert, M., *The Roots of Appeasement* (London, 1966).

Grenville, J. A. S., *Lord Salisbury and Foreign Policy at the Close of the Nineteenth Century* (London, 1970).

Harris, K., *Attlee* (London, 1982).

Haslam, J., *The Soviet Union and the Struggle for Collective Security in Europe, 1933–39* (London, 1984).

Hennesy, P. and Seldon, A. (eds), *Ruling Performance: British governments from Attlee to Thatcher* (Oxford, 1987).

Hinsley, F. H. (ed.), *British Foreign Policy under Sir Edward Grey* (Cambridge, 1977).

Hogan, M. J., *The Marshall Plan: America, Britain and the Reconstruction of Western Europe, 1947–52* (Cambridge, 1987).

Howard, M., *The Continental Commitment* (London, 1972).

Kennedy, P., *The Rise of Anglo-German Antagonism, 1860–1914* (London, 1980).

Kennedy, P., *The Realities Behind Diplomacy: background influences on British external policy, 1865–1980* (London, 1981).

James, R. R., *Anthony Eden* (London, 1986).

Lamb, R., *The Failure of the Eden Government* (London, 1987).

Lewis, J., *Changing Direction: British military planning for post-war strategic defence, 1942–47* (London, 1988).

Louis, W. R., *British Strategy in the Far East, 1919–39* (Oxford, 1971).

Louis, W. R., *The British Empire in the Middle East, 1945–51* (Oxford, 1984).

Louis, W. R. and Bull, H. (eds), *The Special Relationship: Anglo-American Relations since 1945* (Oxford, 1986).

Lowe, C. J., *The Mirage of Power: British Foreign Policy, 1902–22*, 2 vols (London, 1972).

MacDonald, C. A., *The United States, Britain and Appeasement, 1936–39* (London, 1981).

Malone, P., *The British Nuclear Deterrent* (London, 1984).

Marks, S., *The Illusion of Peace: international relations in Europe, 1918–33* (London, 1976).

Martel, G. (ed.), *The Origins of the Second World War Reconsidered: the A. J. P. Taylor debate after twenty five years* (London, 1986).

Medlicott, W. N., *British Foreign Policy since Versailles, 1919–63* (London, 1968).

Middlemas, K., *The Diplomacy of Illusion: the British government and Germany, 1937–39* (London, 1972).

Mommsen, W. J. and Kettenacher, L. (eds), *The Fascist Challenge and the Policy of Appeasement* (London, 1983).

Monger, G. W., *The End of Isolation: British foreign policy, 1900–7* (London, 1963).

Nelson, H. I., *Land and Power: British and allied policy on Germany's frontiers, 1916–19* (London, 1963).

Newman, S., *March 1939: the British Guarantee to Poland* (Oxford, 1976).

Nish, I. H., *The Anglo-Japanese Alliance, 1894–1907* (London, 1966).

Northedge, F. S., *The Troubled Giant: Britain among the great powers, 1916–39* (London, 1966).

Northedge, F. S., *Descent from Power: British Foreign Policy, 1945–73* (London, 1974).

Northedge, F. S. and Wells, A., *Britain and Soviet Communism* (London, 1982).

Orde, A., *Great Britain and International Security* (London, 1978).

Ovendale, R. (ed.), *The Foreign Policy of the British Labour Governments, 1945–51* (Leicester, 1984).

Ovendale, R., *The English-Speaking Alliance, 1945–51* (London, 1985).

Peden, G., *British Rearmament and the Treasury, 1932–39* (Edinburgh, 1979).

Peters, A. R., *Anthony Eden at the Foreign Office, 1931–38* (Aldershot and New York, 1986).

Porter, B., *Britain, Europe and the World, 1850–1952* (London, 1983).

Reynolds, D., *The Creation of the Anglo-American Alliance, 1937–41* (London, 1981).

Riste, O. (ed.), *Western Security: the formative years, 1947–53* (Oslo, 1985).

Robbins, K., *Sir Edward Grey* (London, 1971).

Robins, L. J., *The Reluctant Party: Labour and the EEC, 1961–75* (Ormskirk, 1979).

Rothwell, V., *Britain in the Cold War, 1941–47* (London, 1982).

Schmidt, G., *The Politics and Economics of Appeasement: British foreign policy in the 1930s* (Leamington Spa, 1986).

Shlaim, A. (ed.), *British Foreign Secretaries since 1945* (Newton Abbot, 1977).

Steiner, Z., *The Foreign Office and Foreign Policy, 1898–1914* (Cambridge, 1969).

Steiner, Z., *Britain and the Origins of the First World War* (London, 1977).

Taylor, A. J. P., *English History, 1914–45* (Oxford, 1965).

Ullman, R. H., *Anglo-Soviet Relations, 1917–21*, 3 vols (Princeton, 1961–73).

Waites, N. (ed.), *Troubled Neighbours: Franco-British Relations in the Twentieth Century* (London, 1971).

Watt, D. C., *Personalities and Policies: Studies in the Formulation of British Foreign Policy in the Twentieth Century* (London, 1965).

Watt, D. C., *Succeeding John Bull: America in Britain's Place, 1900–75* (Cambridge, 1984).

Wilson, K., *The Policy of Entente: essays on the determinants of British foreign policy, 1904–14* (Cambridge, 1985).

Wilson, K. (ed.), *British Foreign Secretaries: from the Crimean War to the First World War* (London, 1987).

Young, J. W., *Britain, France and the Unity of Europe, 1945–51* (Leicester, 1984).

Young, J. W. (ed.), *The Foreign Policy of Churchill's Peacetime Administration, 1951–55* (Leicester, 1988).

## ARTICLES

Adamthwaite, A., 'War Origins Again', *Journal of Modern History*, 56 (1984), 100–15.

Adamthwaite, A., 'Britain and the World, 1945–9: the view from the Foreign Office', *International Affairs*, 61 (1985), 223–35.

Adamthwaite, A., 'Overstretched and overstrung: Eden, the Foreign Office and the making of policy, 1951–5', *International Affairs*, 64 (1988), 241–59.

Frazier, R., 'Did Britain start the Cold War? Bevin and the Truman Doctrine', *Historical Journal*, 27 (1984), 715–27.

Hennessy, P. and Laity, M., 'Suez – What the papers say?', *Contemporary Record*, 2 (Spring 1988), 2–5.

Hinds, A. E., 'Sterling and Imperial Preference, 1945–51', *Journal of Imperial and Commonwealth History*, 15 (1987), 148–69.

Kitchen, M., 'Winston Churchill and the Soviet Union during the Second World War', *Historical Journal*, 30 (1987), 415–36.

Little, D., 'Red Scare, 1936: anti-Bolshevism and the origins of British non-intervention in the Spanish Civil War', *Journal of Contemporary History*, 23 (1988), 291–311.

Melissen, J. and Zeeman, B., 'Britain and Western Europe, 1945–51: opportunities lost', *International Affairs*, 63 (1986–7), 81–95.

Peden, G. C., 'A Matter of Timing: the economic background to British foreign policy, 1937–39', *History*, 69 (1984), 15–28.

Watt, D. C., 'Appeasement. The Rise of a Revisionist School', *Political Quarterly*, 36 (1965), 191–213.

Wheeler, N. J., 'British nuclear weapons and Anglo-American relations, 1945–54', *International Affairs*, 62 (1985–6), 71–86.

Young, J. W., 'Churchill's "No" to Europe: the "rejection" of European Union by Churchill's Post-war Government, 1951–52', *Historical Journal*, 28 (1985), 923–37.

# INDEX